Trails of the

SOUTHERN CARIBOO

Trails of the

SOUTHERN CARIBOO

Second Edition

COLIN CAMPBELL

Rocky
Mountain Books
VANCOUVER • VICTORIA • CALGARY

Rocky Mountain Books
#108 – 17665 66A Avenue
Surrey, BC V3S 2A7
www.rmbooks.com

Rocky Mountain Books
PO Box 468
Custer, WA
98240-0468

Library and Archives Canada Cataloguing in Publication

Campbell, Colin, 1941-
    Trails of the southern Cariboo / Colin Campbell.

Previously published under title: Trails of the southern Cariboo.
ISBN 978-1-897522-44-8

    1. Hiking--British Columbia—Cariboo Region—Guidebooks. 2. Trails—British Columbia—Cariboo Region—Guidebooks. 3. Cariboo Region (B.C.)—Guidebooks. I. Campbell, Colin, 1941-   . Trails of the southern Cariboo. II. Title.

GV199.44.C22C37 2009   917.11'75045   C2008-907155-7

Library of Congress Control Number: 2009920183

Front cover photo: Farwell Ridge
Back cover photo: Pete Kitchen Lake

Printed in Canada

Rocky Mountain Books acknowledges the financial support for its publishing program from the Government of Canada through the Book Publishing Industry Development Program (BPIDP), Canada Council for the Arts, and the province of British Columbia through the British Columbia Arts Council and the Book Publishing Tax Credit.

Disclaimer

The actions described in this book may be considered inherently dangerous activities. Individuals undertake these activities at their own risk. The information put forth in this guide has been collected from a variety of sources and is not guaranteed to be completely accurate or reliable. Many conditions and some information may change owing to weather and numerous other factors beyond the control of the authors and publishers. Individual climbers and/or hikers must determine the risks, use their own judgment, and take full responsibility for their actions. Do not depend on any information found in this book for your own personal safety. Your safety depends on your own good judgment based on your skills, education, and experience.

    It is up to the users of this guidebook to acquire the necessary skills for safe experiences and to exercise caution in potentially hazardous areas. The authors and publishers of this guide accept no responsibility for your actions or the results that occur from another's actions, choices, or judgments. If you have any doubt as to your safety or your ability to attempt anything described in this guidebook, do not attempt it.

Contents

Introduction

Often referred to in tourist literature as Canada's "True West," the Cariboo–Chilcotin is a vast and varied region covering the central portion of British Columbia. With a tiny population and a huge landmass comprising a variety of subregions and topographies, it is still very much a frontier area. The "True West" designation relates in part to the area's colourful past, particularly to the heady days of the 1850s Cariboo Gold Rush. Today the Western image lives on in the ranching business, which along with forestry, tourism, log-home building and mining, remains one of the economic mainstays of the region.

When it comes to actually defining the boundaries of the Cariboo, we find a degree of vagueness. Some publications cite Prince George as the northern boundary, while others place the ceiling farther south at Quesnel. The southern boundary is variously attached to the villages of Clinton, Cache Creek and Lillooet. There is consensus at least on the western and eastern boundaries: the Fraser River in the west and the rolling hills of the Cariboo Mountains eastward define those borders. In recent years the Cariboo Tourist Association has included in its publications a map that consistently shows the northern boundary as just north of the city of Quesnel, and the southern limit at Lillooet.

The Chilcotin refers to that great territory on the west flank of the Cariboo stretching all the way from the Fraser River to the Coast Mountains.

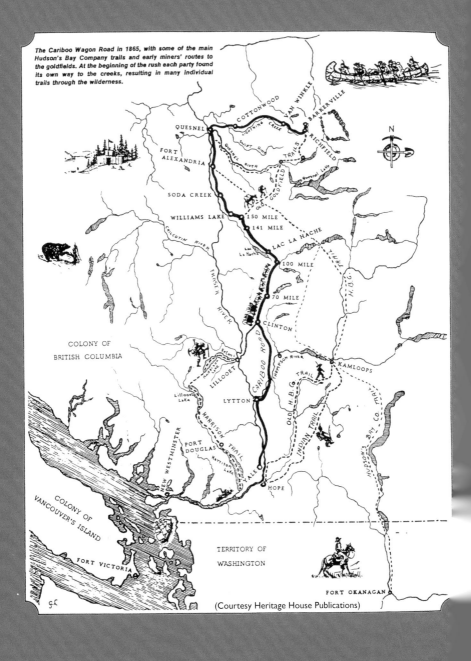

The Cariboo Wagon Road in 1865, with some of the main Hudson's Bay Company trails and early miners' routes to the goldfields. At the beginning of the rush each party found its own way to the creeks, resulting in many individual trails through the wilderness.

COTTONWOOD
VAN WINKLE
BARKERVILLE
QUESNEL
Lightning Creek
RICHFIELD
FORT ALEXANDRIA
Quesnel River
Swift River
GOLDFIELD TRAILS
Quesnel Lake
SODA CREEK
WILLIAMS LAKE
150 MILE
141 MILE
Chilcotin River
LAC LA HACHE
Lac La Hache
100 MILE
FRASER RIVER
70 MILE
CLINTON
COLONY OF BRITISH COLUMBIA
Seton
Anderson
CARIBOO ROAD
Thompson River
KAMLOOPS
OLD H.B.C. TRAIL
LILLOOET
Lillooet Lake
LYTTON
INDIAN TRAIL
HARRISON TRAIL
HUDSON BAY CO. TRAIL
PORT DOUGLAS
Harrison Lake
NEW WESTMINSTER
YALE
HOPE
COLONY OF VANCOUVER'S ISLAND
FORT VICTORIA

N

TERRITORY OF WASHINGTON

FORT OKANAGAN

(Courtesy Heritage House Publications)

The Names Cariboo–Chilcotin

The differing opinions as to the boundaries of the Cariboo are matched by a corresponding variety of options relating to the place name. Tall stories aside, the most likely explanation of its origin, the one most commonly agreed on is that of a corruption of "caribou," a reference to the herds of woodland caribou that once roamed west of the Fraser River and that were remarked upon by pioneers and explorers, some of whom may have been spelling-challenged.

The Chilcotin takes its name from the First Nations people of the region, "the people of the Chilco," who, along with the Shuswap people, constitute the majority of the population. "Chilco" translates variously as "blue water" and "young man's river."

Scope of this Guide

To include all of the possible hikes in an area as vast as described would require several guidebooks. I have chosen to limit this book to a manageable chunk of the region, specifically to the south-central Cariboo, as well as an eastern section of the Chilcotin. This amounts to a corridor stretching from the Chilcotin River in the northwest to just beyond Likely in the northeast. At the southern end, the corridor stretches from the western limits of the Marble Range to the Mahood area in the southeast. The criterion attached to each hike is that it should be within reasonable reach of the area's three main population centres: Williams Lake, 100 Mile House and Clinton.

Changes Since the First Edition

In addition to the inclusion of 15 new trails to this edition, most of the earlier described trails have been revisited in order to verify or update information and to refresh photographs.

The access point for some of the trails in the Marble Range has changed, and two trails from the first edition have been deleted.

Climate Change

The most significant change in the decade since the first edition appeared has occurred as a result of climate change and correspondingly warmer winters. The landscape of the region has been profoundly altered in many areas as a result of the western pine beetle infestation that has seen huge areas of lodgepole pine and smaller tracts of pondorosa pine decimated. Formerly vibrant green forest reduced to a skeletal brown. Whether these changes are purely cyclical in nature or accelerated by human activity, the effects are dramatic.

On a brighter note, in some locations, especially in the 100 Mile House area, young aspens are filling in where the pine has died, and as they mature they will restore the leafy beauty of those areas and add even more colour in the fall.

Topography

Two of the three main ecoregions of the Cariboo–Chilcotin fall within the scope of this guide: the Fraser Plateau and the Columbia Mountains and Highlands. A third, the Fraser Basin, begins midway between Williams Lake and Quesnel and extends northward. With the exception of the Quesnel and Horsefly Lakes areas, all of the trails described are located on the Fraser Plateau, a subdivision of the Interior Plateau, which occupies nearly one quarter of the landmass of British Columbia. The Fraser Plateau is a basically flat to gently rolling region lying between elevations of 900 m and 1650 m. The plateau changes gradually from a flat surface underlain by volcanic bedrock in the central western part, to rolling uplands and rounded hills in the eastern half. At its lower southwest quarter, the steep limestone ridges of the Marble Range are included as a subunit because of their small area: only 35 km long and 15 km wide. Evidence of substantial past volcanic activity can be seen throughout the region in the form of volcanic plugs, lava layers in canyons and on the sides of ridges. Volcanic cinders are found all over.

As the volcanoes made their contribution to shaping the region, ice also left its mark. The great ice sheets that once covered this land also created much of its beauty. Thousands of lakes and kettle ponds dot the landscape, and long stretches of wetlands attract large numbers of migratory birds and wildfowl.

The eastern part of the Chilcotin is an ecological jewel characterized by extensive grasslands: one of the only remaining intact bluebunch wheatgrass grasslands in North America and the largest remaining area of North America's intermountain grassland system. The area is dominated by the deep trench of the Fraser River and its spectacular bench lands.

Climate

The Coast Mountains act as a barrier to the moist westerly airflow, rendering the region much dryer than the coast. The Cariboo's climate is characterized by warm summers that are prone to hot dry spells. Winters have been noticeably milder in recent years. Snow begins to fall after mid-November, usually. Spring is short, with the ice leaving the lakes around mid- to late April. Leaves begin to appear on the trees mid-May.

The Chilcotin has a continental temperate climate and tends to be very dry, with nearly desert-like conditions.

My preferred time for hiking either region is spring or fall at lower elevations, when the bugs have either not yet appeared or have been zapped by early frost. Snow can be encountered in the Marble peaks in late September and generally lingers through June.

Wildlife

The Fraser Plateau supports a wide diversity of animal life in a wide range of habitats. Among the larger mammals, mule deer are plentiful and are widely distributed throughout. There are significant numbers of moose, and California bighorn sheep roam the valleys and arid benchlands of the Fraser and Chilcotin rivers. Black bears are plentiful and grizzlies are to be found in the mountains north and east of Hendrix Lake, as well as in

The 83 Mile House, built 1862. (Image courtesy of Royal BC Museum, BC Archives).

the Cariboo Mountains. Fox and coyote are abundant. Wolf are around but not abundant. Shyer creatures, such as fisher, lynx and bobcat, make their home here, and cougars are reported quite frequently. In recent years badgers, likely lured by warmer winters, have been sighted in the Cariboo, and efforts are underway to track and record their numbers.

The thousands of lakes and long chains of wetlands attract large numbers and many species of migratory birds and wildfowl. Ducks Unlimited has been active in the region for over 40, years undertaking extensive restoration projects aimed at stabilizing and boosting the wildfowl population and encouraging other species. In all, the region boasts an estimated 514,000 acres of wetlands.

The raptor population is a healthy one and includes bald and golden eagles, osprey and many species of hawk. The largest of the migratory bird species found in the region is the sandhill crane. Often sighted on rangeland meadows, these ancient birds are very sensitive to intrusion and tend not to wait around to be photographed.

The grasslands of the Chilcotin is home to many of the continent's most vulnerable and endangered species, including the burrowing owl, Lewis's woodpecker, long-billed curlew, American avocet and sharp-tailed grouse. Some 70 km west of Williams Lake, White Pelican Provincial Park is home to British Columbia's sole nesting colony of red-listed American white pelicans. The birds can be spotted feeding on Williams Lake and other lakes nearby as they migrate north or south in the spring or fall.

Flora

Plant life in the region is equally widely diversified, ranging from cactus and sagebrush in the dry Chilcotin to coastal-type vegetation in the wetter eastern reaches. Much of the land is (or was) covered in lodgepole pine interspersed with trembling aspen, spruce and Douglas fir. Farther east, toward the mountains, western red cedar and hemlock reflect higher precipitation. Pockets of cottonwood and paper birch are found at different locations, while Engelmann spruce and subalpine fir mark the higher elevations.

In alpine and subalpine areas and the less arid meadows east of the Fraser, where the cattle haven't cropped too heavily, there are fine displays of wildflowers. At higher elevations, such as the Eureka Peak meadows, the summer floral display can be spectacular, with meadow and streamside displays of sunburst yarrow, harebell, gentian, potentilla, columbine and campanula among many others. In spring, in the middle and upper grasslands west of the Fraser, meadows and hillsides clothed in a dazzling sunshine-yellow blanket of arrowroot balsam greet those lucky hikers who venture out there.

A Brief History of the Region

Prior to 1858, what is referred to today as the Cariboo was known only to the First Nations peoples, the fur traders and a few hardy explorers. The only existing roads were the hunting and trading trails of the Shuswap and those of the fur brigades.

In February of 1858 all of this changed. Word raced around the port of San Francisco that the Hudson's Bay steamship *Otter* had arrived with 800 ounces of gold from the Fraser River. That news started a stampede of gold seekers northward to the sandbars of the lower Fraser with some venturing farther north up the Quesnel River to the Cariboo.

In the fall of 1860, "Doc" Keithly and his companions discovered gold in a Cariboo stream they named Keithly Creek, near the present-day community of Likely. Discoveries on other creeks followed, culminating in the most famous of all by William "Dutch Bill" Dietz and his party on a stretch of Williams Creek between Richfield and Barkerville. As fast as fact and fancy can fly, news of the discoveries in the Cariboo brought miners and would-be miners by the thousands, pouring into the Wells–Barkerville area, their appetites whetted by the announcement that the output of gold for 1861 totalled $2.7-million.

By May 1862, some 6,000 miners entered the Cariboo over the most forbidding territory. The immediate result was a shortage of food and supplies, since there was no alternative to packing stuff in individually over primitive and dangerous trails.

Aware of the need to get supplies into the region and reduce the cost of transportation, Governor James Douglas assigned the Royal Engineers the task of constructing roads, with some of the work delegated in turn to independent contractors. One such route started on the lower Fraser linking Harrison and Lillooet and bypassing the Fraser Canyon. In the summer of 1862, work got underway to extend this trail from Lillooet to Clinton and beyond to Alexandria. Contractors on the Cariboo Trail were paid per mile and required a post at every mile of construction, with Lillooet designated as mile zero. Along the way, every 10 or 15 miles, entrepreneurs established roadhouses (mile houses) to serve crews and travellers alike.

Although many of the original roadhouses did not last, some developed into active communities bearing the name of their location along the Cariboo Road.

The 100 Mile Roadhouse, built 1861. (Image courtesy of Royal BC Museum, BC Archives).

Thus we have locations today such as 70, 100, 108 and 150 Mile Houses. A number of creeks and ranches along the Gold Rush Route of Highway 97 are named according to their location at a mile marker. Very few of the original roadhouses remain, most having succumbed to deterioration or fire.

The Trails

I have hiked, biked or skied all of the trails listed and designated them as easy, moderate or advanced. Except for the occasional mountain trail, there are few advanced trails. A few hikes or biking routes have been designated moderate/advanced mainly because of their length, the presence of tough hilly sections, or an element of bushwhacking. The scree slopes of the Marble Mountains require careful treading. The majority of trails listed, however, are rated easy/moderate, since much of the terrain is meadowland or rolling-hill country.

With the exception of loop trails, where the total distance and suggested completion times are given, distances and times have been calculated one way from the starting point. In most instances this refers to the trailhead, but in others an access road may be included if it is to be walked or biked after parking.

Elevation and elevation gain or loss are provided where appropriate.

Maps

For the majority of trails, the maps were created using overlays on standard 1:250 000 topographic maps, most of which are considerably dated (the topo maps for this region are of 1970s vintage.) More recent trail additions were plotted on commercially available base maps. For the ski trails, I have used maps provided by the Forest Service or by the resort or ski club responsible for the trails.

Every effort has been made to ensure accuracy, but it is recognized that even with the most careful checking and proofreading, the occasional error can still find its way in. If you should find one, be understanding. Pat it on the head – don't scold it. If it is significant, let me know.

Acknowledgements

My thanks to my various hiking and biking partners for their company and their patience as we stopped and started while waiting for the sun to peek through and make photographs possible.

Thanks also to the following people for their input and assistance: Barrie Bolton, for his invaluable work in preparing the maps for the new trails; Peter Crawshay, who was very helpful in explaining the intricacies of GPS to a hopeless Luddite and owner of the world's most fickle computer; and Murray Helmer, who kindly loaned me a camera at a critical time. My thanks also to the staffs of the South Cariboo Visitor Centre in 100 Mile House and the Williams Lake Visitor Centre for their helpful assistance.

Photographs

With the exception of those credited, all photographs were taken by the author and remain the property of the author.

Area Map

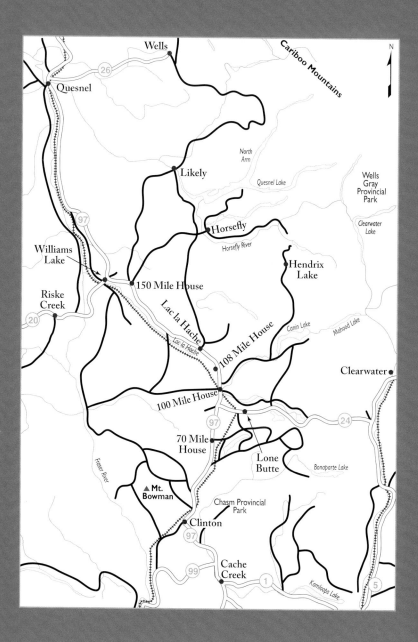

Trails + Routes

Hat Creek and the Marble Range

The Hat Creek Ranch

This historic landmark, located 11 km north of Cache Creek at the junction of Highway 97 and Highway 99 South is such a great place to gain a feel for the Cariboo's colourful past that it justifies a mention in this trail guide and well merits a visit.

The ranch had its beginnings in 1861, when Donald McLean, chief trader of the Hudson's Bay Company at Kamloops, retired and brought his family and cattle to Hat Creek. Within a year he had built a log structure that became known to travellers as "McLean Station." Following McLean's death three years later in a skirmish with Chilcotin warriors, the property passed to his widow. Sophia McLean subsequently sold to George Dunne, who transformed the house into a hotel. The property changed hands a number of times more before being acquired by Steve Tingley of the BC Express Stageline in 1894. Thus began the most active and exciting period for the ranch. Tingley made the hotel the first stopping house for his stage and freight business out of Ashcroft and added a kitchen and more guest rooms, creating one of the most elegant hotels between Yale and Barkerville.

On the grounds, Tingley added the BX barn to house the lighter stage-coach horses, a freight horse barn for the heavier teams and a blacksmith shop.

Subsequent owners expanded the ranch to 20,000 acres and added a general store and sawmill. In 1952 a new residence was built and the hotel converted into a bunkhouse for the cowhands. The ranch became the property of BC Hydro in 1977. Today it is managed by the BC Heritage Trust and has become a popular visitor attraction on the doorstep of the Cariboo.

I. BONAPARTE RIDGE, HAT CREEK

Easy/moderate hike
Distance 1+ km
Elevation gain 150 m
Map 92 I/13 Cache Creek

Access: From the Hat Creek Ranch parking lot, cross the road (Highway 99 South) and note the ranch road running north. To the left, on other side of the gate, is a trail winding up to the top of the ridge.

The trail to the top of the ridge is short and steep but easy-going. The terrain is desert-like with sagebrush bunchgrass and cactus. The ridge presents great views of the Bonaparte River Valley north and the Hat Creek Ranch valley south. Continuing westward along the ridge opens up more hiking possibilities, albeit with light bushwhacking, along a series of animal paths.

The Village of Clinton

It is from this attractively situated forestry and ranching community of 600 plus that we access the Marble Range and its great ridge hiking. Clinton itself is worth a stop. It has a colourful history associated with the gold rush and has retained something of the flavour of those times in its Western-style decoration. Of particular interest is the village museum, itself a museum piece, with its collection of artifacts from the days of the Cariboo Wagon Road; the former Palace Hotel, built in 1897 and now a residence; and the Clinton Emporium, with its bric-a-brac from the last century and before. A good base from which to explore the Marbles, Clinton offers motel, B&B, camping and nearby guest accommodation.

The Marble Range

Considered a subunit of the Fraser Plateau, geologically the Marble Range is part of a limestone unit, the Marble Canyon Formation, which extends as a narrow elongate belt from Spences Bridge northwest to Jesmond. The range takes its name from Marble Canyon near Pavilion Lake along Highway 99 South. The highest peaks are at the northern end, where the more arid climate renders the limestone more resistant to weathering. The area has been assigned provincial park status, but with the exception of a few horse trails constructed by local outfitters, hiking trails, where they exist, are fairly primitive. Once you find your way up, however, you are looking at some of the best hiking in the Cariboo.

Limestone formations, Marble Range.

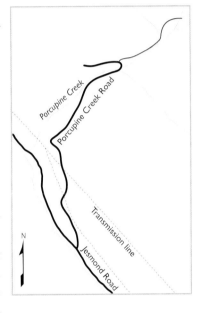

2. LIME RIDGE (EAST)

Easy/moderate hike
Distance 5 km
Duration 2 hours
Elevation gain 650 m
Map 92 P/4 Clinton

Access: From Clinton, take the Kelly Lake Road at the south end of the village for 16 km and turn right on the unpaved Jesmond Road. At about 5.5 km look for a road on the right with a stop sign. The sign will be facing away from you. This is Porcupine Road, although there is no sign indicating this. From here it is 5.3 km to the trailhead.

Porcupine Road is a dirt road better at certain times of the year than others. A high-clearance vehicle is a must at any time. To pinpoint the trailhead, look for a corral on the right at around 4.5 km. Continue past the corral for another 800 m to the stream. On the right are signs of an old campfire. The trail begins here and winds its way through the forest above the stream for 3 km before crossing the stream and continuing up through a gully. At the top of the gully, turn right. From here the trail climbs steeply for under a kilometre to the ridge. Once on top, you can continue hiking along the ridge to right or left and enjoy great views of weathered limestone bluffs and deep, forested valleys.

Looking west from Lime Ridge to Edge Hills Park.

In the background, Edge Hills and the Camelsfoot Range.

3. LIME RIDGE VIA MINING ROAD

Moderate hike
Distance 4 km
Duration 2 hours
Maximum elevation 2165 m
Elevation gain 705 m
Map 92 P/4 Clinton

Access: See Lime Ridge East, hike #2. Drive 15 km along Jesmond Road to a clearing on the left-hand side. There is a creek running through, and the area on the right has been logged. Park on the left and cross the road. Walk east 100 m to a dirt road heading north under the power lines.

Not the most attractive approach to Lime Ridge, and accessing the ridge is a bit of a challenge. Once you're there, however, the views are great and the ridge walking is fine.

Before crossing under the power lines you will encounter a service road running west to east across the trail. Stay to the left until the next intersecting road branching under the power lines, at which point go right, heading directly toward the peaks. At one point along the way you should encounter indications of former limestone-mining activity.

A few hundred metres from its end, the mining road takes a curve uphill westward and comes to an end against a rocky outcrop. A narrow path curves around the base of the rock and begins to climb in a northeasterly direction through the forest. When the trail becomes indistinct, continue heading uphill northeast toward the base of the bluffs across a couple of

27

small scree slopes. To access the ridge from this point requires choosing either a moderately difficult climb up a chimney or crossing an extensive scree slope running down from the ridge and then approaching the ridge from the east side.

Alternative approaches are likely possible; it's a matter of finding them.

Atop Lime Ridge.

Heading east on Lime Ridge. Porcupine Creek hike.

4. MAD DOG MOUNTAIN

Moderate hike, some bushwhacking
Distance 7 km
Duration 3 hours
Maximum elevation 2070 m
Elevation gain 725 m
Map 92 P/4 Clinton

Access: From Clinton via Kelly Lake Road to Jesmond turnoff. About 19 km along Jesmond road, watch for a concrete house foundation on the right. Walk right or left of the foundation toward the trees to the trailhead.

This peak, just east of Mount Bowman, supposedly resembles the lower canine tooth, hence the name. The hike involves some reconnoitering and bushwhacking, but the panorama from the top, west to Mount Bowman and the Fraser River trench, is worth the scramble.

The approach track to the right of the foundation has become quite overgrown and may be hard to locate. After a short walk through the woods, however, the trail becomes visible crossing a clearing and resuming on the other side of the power lines heading northeast toward the notch between Mad Dog Mountain and Lime Ridge. Foundation Creek is just to the right and the trail follows close to it. Around the 1 km mark the path enters a little meadow where it partially disappears owing to flooding and vegetation growth. Pick up the trail on the other side and continue until, at a junction, about

4 km along, the Mad Dog Mountain trail splits left of the main trail. Heading now in a northwesterly direction uphill through forest, the trail is well-defined to start then disappears and reappears until becoming indistinguishable from other horse and animal trails.

It is at this point the bushwhacking begins. Mad Dog Mountain is to the left, the northwest, and it is a matter of picking a way through the trees and scrub until you encounter rock then simply taking the line of least resistance to get above the treeline. The summit is marked with an old claim marker from the Continental Lime Company.

Returning from Mad Dog Mountain.

5. *LIME RIDGE (WEST)*

Easy hike
Distance 6 km
Duration 3 hours
Maximum Elevation 2165 m
Elevation gain 820 m
Map 92 P/4 Clinton

Access: See Mad Dog Mountain, hike #4.

The hike to the ridge has much to offer by way of wildflowers and terrific views of the surrounding peaks and ridges. Lime Ridge is 5.5 km long, as wide as a playing field for much of its length and invites exploration in all directions. It is about a three-hour hike to the ridge, but once there it is likely you will want to continue along it for a way before heading back.

To begin with, the Lime Ridge trail and the Mad Dog Mountain trail are one until a point about 4 km along where the latter splits off left. From this junction, continue upward in a northeasterly direction with the creek – sometimes visible, sometimes vanishing underground – on the right. The trail winds through forest, gradually narrowing into a ravine rich in plant life. Look for aster, yellow monkey flower, wild orchid, alpine columbine, hairbell and wild gooseberry among the variety of flowers and shrubs. Stay on the main trail bearing northeast through a narrow canyon-like section then into a more open area with rhododendron bushes and willows. At this point, be aware of a trail that veers to the right, or southeasterly. Here the creek has made one of its underground vanishings. Follow the creekbed, and when you reach the saddle, search for the path on the right-hand side of the scree slope. This begins the steepest section of the trail, a 2-km grunt to the western extremity of the ridge.

It is advisable at this point to take your bearings and note for the return trip where you came up onto the ridge, as weather changes can sometimes make for orienteering problems on the unmarked trails. Also, other than a possible snowmelt patch, you are unlikely to find water on the ridge.

Windswept junipers, Lime Ridge.

Heading east on Lime Ridge. Porcupine Creek hike.

6. MOUNT BOWMAN

Moderate hike

Distance 7 km

Duration 3 hours

Maximum elevation 2243 m

Elevation gain 900 m

Map 92 P/4 Clinton

Access: 22 km along Jesmond Road and 1 km before the Circle H Mountain Lodge, look for a cleared area on the right just as you round the bend in the road. The road climbs to the left under the power line. Unless you have a vehicle with high clearance you should park at the high spot and walk the remaining 1 km to the next parking spot at the bottom of the hill.

Mount Bowman, because of its location near several guest ranches, is by far the most popular of the Marble Range hikes. The route is straightforward: through forest to begin then through alpine meadow to below the summit. The final stretch, however, is steep and requires careful negotiating due to the loose nature of the fragmented limestone. The peak presents outstanding views to the Coast Mountains and the Cayoosh Mountains due west. Mission Ridge and the Camelsfoot Range lie to the southwest.

From the parking area head left across the stream exiting the pond and then right on the dirt road. This is the start of the Mount Bowman trail. From here the trail wends its way through the forest with a stream on your right until, about 4 km along, you arrive at a clearing by the stream with the remains of campfires. Here the path splits left to Mount Bowman or continues straight ahead to Wildhorse Ridge and Mount Kerr. Heading left, the trail climbs through a wooded section with the stream on the right to begin with and on the left as we climb. After this we cross an open boggy area then traverse an alpine meadow to the base of the mountain. A number of scree-covered paths lead from here to a larger scree slope from which it is a short steep scramble to the ridge and from there to the peak.

7. WILD HORSE RIDGE

Moderate hike
Distance 9 km
Duration 3 hours
Maximum elevation 2125 m
Elevation gain 780 m
Map 92 P/4 Clinton

Access: See Mt. Bowman, hike #6.

This is a fairly lengthy hike in itself and any additional exploring of the inviting ridges on either side can make for a long day. An alternative is to tent and use this as a base from which to explore the curving northwest part of the ridge and the eastern section leading to Mount Kerr. Carry water, as you are unlikely to find any on top in the summer.

From the ridges there are spectacular panoramas in all directions.

The first 4-km section of the trail is the same as in the hike to

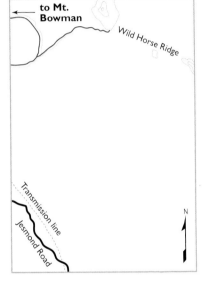

Mount Bowman. At the point where the Bowman trail turns left, however, the path to Wild Horse Ridge heads uphill following the stream much of the way and is easily followed to the subalpine. There are good sheltered locations on the saddle if you choose to tent. From the saddle there is great ridge-walking to right or left. The ridge to the right of the saddle leading to Mount Kerr is more rugged. It is advisable to take note of your bearings if you head in the direction of Mount Kerr, as on the return, the trail can be hard to spot where it exits the trees onto the ridge.

8. MOUNT KERR

SegmentModerate/advanced hike
Duration 2-day backpack
Maximum elevation 2165 m
Elevation gain 820 m
Map 92 P/4 Clinton

Access: See Wild Horse Ridge, hike #7

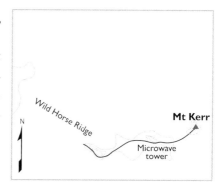

Mount Kerr is located east of the Wild Horse Ridge saddle. The peak itself is hidden from most points along the ridge, but a good reference point is provided by the clearly visible microwave tower. Mount Kerr lies less than a kilometre farther along, about 5 km from the saddle. The hike from this point, some of it along narrow ridges, takes about three hours and is considered the most spectacular in the Marble Range. There are wonderful rainbow-coloured scree slopes on the south side of the ridge and spurs of jagged limestone cliffs running off to the north. Getting to the peak after leaving the microwave tower entails some tricky scrambling. Ropes are not essential, but it is recommended you bring them. From the top, there is an uninterrupted view eastward across Green Lake all the way to the Cariboo Mountains. The views from the microwave tower are just as spectacular, should you choose not to continue beyond this.

Waking up to snow, Mt. Kerr.

Hat Creek and Marble Range

35

9. *BIG BAR LAKE TRAIL*

Easy hike
Distance 4 km
Duration 1 hour
Map 92 P/4 Clinton

Access: 42 km northwest of Clinton via Kelly Lake and Jesmond roads or 34 km via Big Bar Road 13 km north of Clinton.

A very pleasant signed scenic walk along the lakeshore, around some attractive woodlands and along a scooped-up 500-m-long esker affording beautiful mountain and lake views and wildlife spotting. The trail is in a popular, well-appointed provincial park with several campsites.

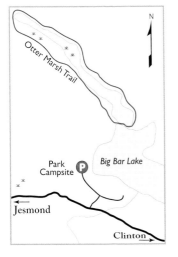

On the Big Bar trail.

Chasm to Mount Begbie

10. *PAINTED CHASM*

Easy walks, mountain biking
Distance 1+ km
Duration 0.25 hour
Map 92 P/3 Loon Lake

Access: Fifteen km north of Clinton the road to Painted Chasm intersects Highway 97 on the right. It is a 7-km drive to Chasm Provincial Park from here. From the north, 50 km south of 100 Mile House, a directional sign on the left indicates Painted Chasm. It is a 3-km drive from there.

Some 300 m deep, Painted Chasm is the central feature of Chasm Provincial Park. The name refers to the mineral-pigmented, multi-layered nature of the canyon walls, built up over thousands of years by the successive

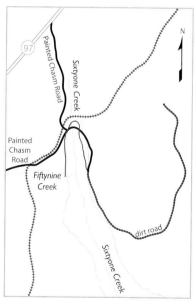

flows of lava that, layer by layer, built up the Fraser Plateau. The gorge itself is reminiscent of the canyon at Helmecken Falls in Wells Gray Park, though it lacks the latter's spectacular waterfall. Indeed, the two share the same origin. Around 10,000 years ago, when the last ice age ended, silt-laden ice waters from the Fraser River system assaulted cracks in the lava, eroding the basaltic rock and expanding the cracks sometimes by thousands of metres. The Painted Chasm was eroded 8,000 m in length and 60 m across.

Despite park expansion, trail development remains very limited. From the parking lot, a trail veers left around the head of the gorge across Sixtyone Creek, providing limited access to the east side. It is possible to continue beyond the fenced park boundaries on this side, however, by continuing alongside a wire fence for about 500 m to where it intersects a dirt road running north–south. This road meanders through the forest forever, it seems. It is not a particularly interesting road in itself. What it does offer, for the first 2 km, are great views across the west wall of the canyon to the Marble Mountains. Mountain biking would be the best way to explore this route.

South from the parking lot, a chainlink safety fence extends the first 500 m, after which walkers have worn a path another 500 m or so to a tree-choked waterfall on Fiftynine Creek, which plummets to the canyon floor. Venturing beyond the fenced boundaries can be dangerous and requires great caution.

The Painted Chasm looking southeast.

Chasm view looking southeast.

11. *LOCH LOMOND*

Easy hike, bike
Distance 8 km
Duration 1.5-hour hike
Map 92 P/6 Green Lake

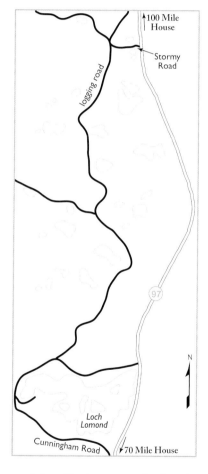

Access: From the south, 20 km north of 70 Mile House, turn left onto Stormy Road and park at the pull-in area on the left. From the north, at 30 km south of 100 Mile House, turn right on Stormy Road.

This fascinating landscape, dotted with ponds and strewn with large, orange, lichen-stained boulders, has long intrigued visitors. Like so many others, I had driven past the area countless times heading elsewhere, vowing to stop and explore it some day, but I was intimidated by fences. It came as a pleasant surprise, then, to learn that the area is leased Crown land and, as an added bonus, has rich historical connections.

Mountain biking is the best way to travel the logging roads to the ponds. Just 500 m along Stormy Road from the parking area, turn left at the 391.37 logging road sign. The latter stretch of road is part of the original Cariboo Wagon Road. Follow this road to the 391.40 sign about 4 km along and stay left.

It is another 4 km to Loch Lomond on the left. The areas to be explored on foot or by bike are the north and south sides of the lake and its bays. The area west of the lake is ranch land belonging to the Cunningham family, generations of whom have run cattle there.

Behind the Name Loch Lomond

As one might suspect, there is a Scottish connection. In 1862 Scottish-born Sergeant John McMurphy of the Royal Engineers pre-empted 160 acres of land located between the 73 and 74 mileposts. McMurphy had been in charge of a crew of more than two hundred road builders constructing a stretch of the Cariboo Wagon Road. When the Royal Engineers disbanded in 1863, McMurphy took up the land. Originally he named the lake on the property "Sergeant's Lake," but soon after changed it to the present Loch Lomond. Whether he was inspired by Scottish patriotism or whimsy is not known. The lake itself, really not much more than a large alkaline pond, bears no resemblance to its famous Scottish counterpart. However, looking across it to the distant peaks of the Marble Range on a beautiful spring or fall evening, it is easy to appreciate what might have prompted the good sergeant's nostalgia.

McMurphy went on to build a roadhouse at the southern end of the lake. The hostelry acquired a reputation up and down the Cariboo Road for good food and great hospitality. The venture did not last beyond 1865, however, when newly discovered riches elsewhere drew the miners away and McMurphy was forced to sell, leaving Loch Lomond that same year for New Westminster. No trace of the old roadhouse remains today.

Loch Lomond from Hwy 97. The Marble Range in the background.

12. *CARIBOO WAGON ROAD, 83 MILE HOUSE*

Easy hike
Distance 4 km
Duration 1 hour
Map 92 P/6 Bonaparte Lake

Access: From 100 Mile House, drive 29 km south on Highway 97 to the 83 Mile House Farm Equipment Museum on the right, 2 km south of Begbie Summit. Park by the entrance.

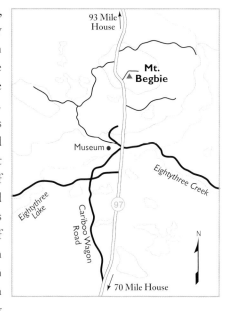

Snaking through the woods between 83 Mile House and 70 Mile House to the west of the highway, are some of the very few uninterrupted stretches of the original 1860s Cariboo Wagon Road. One of these lengths of trail runs from the 83 Mile House Museum with its original gold rush era outbuildings and amazing collection of old farm machinery, wagons and buggies, to Bullock Road, some 4 km south. The old road runs entirely through forest and has narrowed to a trail with the encroachment of vegetation.

The road leading to the 1920s homestead (the original 83 Mile House, dating back to 1864, burned down), is also part of the old Cariboo Road. The trailhead, however, is a little farther along, at a bridge crossing the stream to the left of the homestead. The bridge gets washed out periodically due to the activity of beavers. While this is public access, walkers should make themselves known to the museum's owners, Ray and Vi Young, a genial couple with a wealth of knowledge about the area's colourful past.

13. BEGBIE FORESTRY LOOKOUT

Easy hike
Distance 250 m
Maximum elevation 1269 m
Elevation gain 50 m
Map 92 P/6 Bonaparte Lake

Access: From 100 mile House, 27 km south on Highway 97 at Begbie Summit. Note the sign on the left, "Lookout Road." Park and walk the short trail to the forestry lookout.

While the lookout, from a geological and historical perspective plus its terrific 360-degree vista, is well worth the short clamber to the top, the hiker will want more. To make it a full day, I suggest combining Begbie with a visit to the 83 Mile House Farm Equipment Museum 2 km downhill, and while there, walk the section of the original Cariboo Wagon Road described in hike #12.

There has been a Forest Service fire lookout at this location since 1923, although the current building is not original. The information board at the base states that the tower offers visibility over some 9 million acres of Cariboo forest. The summit was named for the redoubtable gold-rush-era judge Matthew Baillie Begbie.

The Buttes – Lakes Area

Lone Butte and Huckleberry Butte

In an otherwise flattish landscape, the butte at Lone Butte stands out like a rocky fist. A plug of lava that cooled in the opening of a small volcano or vent, the butte is worth the short easy climb to the top for geological reasons alone but also for the panoramic view it offers. A little farther on, Huckleberry Butte, with its heavy covering of trees and bush, has a less dramatic appearance but like its sister butte reveals scattered evidence of the massive forces that millions of years ago created the Fraser Plateau. As neither hike is lengthy, both can easily be accommodated in a morning.

The Community of Lone Butte

Lone Butte is located east of 100 Mile House and can be reached from the south via Highway 24, or from the north via Horse Lake Road or by Highway 24.

You wouldn't think, looking at its one-block main street today, that this sleepy little community was a bustling centre in the early 1900s. Construction of the Pacific Great Eastern Railway from Vancouver to Prince George brought hundreds of railway workers to the area in 1914. Later, Lone Butte became a centre for shipping cattle until truck transportation gradually replaced rail and the stockyards closed. Following this, the town experienced another upswing in business and population as forestry attracted workers to numerous small mills. Once again, however, the relative boom was followed by bust as economics dictated the mills' closure in the 1970s.

Today, Lone Butte is holding its own thanks to its location as gateway to the scenic Interlakes District, with its many fishing and holiday resorts. Worth a visit in Lone Butte is the restored Pacific Great Eastern Railway water tower.

14. *LONE BUTTE*

Short, easy climb
Distance 1 km
Duration 0.25 hour
Maximum elevation 1235 m
Elevation gain 75 m
Map 92 P/11 100 Mile House

Access: On Highway 24, continue through the village less than 1 km to where the Horse Lake Road intersects on the left. On the gravel road just left of the intersection, turn right, park and walk to the right. The final 15 metres is a rocky scramble requiring caution.

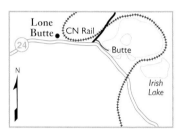

From the butte, looking west to the community of Lone Butte. Note the beetle-killed pines.

15. HUCKLEBERRY BUTTE

Short, easy climb
Distance 1.5 km
Duration 0.5 hour
Elevation gain 85 m
Map 92 P/11 100 Mile House

Access: Via Highway 24, 6 km past Lone Butte, look for Holmes Road on the right. Continue for one more km, park and cross Highway 24 to the trailhead on the left, indicated by the Ministry of Forests and Lands sign advising "Cattle at large, please close the gate."

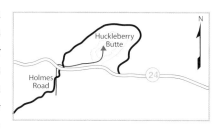

Horse Lake from Huckleberry Butte.

This is a more pleasurable walk than the brief scramble up Lone Butte. The trail climbs through forest, with tiger lilies, arnica and lupine providing colour to the underbrush. While Lone Butte is not a volcanic core, the volcanic cinders and breccia along the way attest to the butte's volcanic past. From the summit, on a clear day, the distant summits of the Trophy Mountains and Dunn Peak are visible to the east.

16. OLSEN'S BUTTE

Easy hike
Distance 1 km
Duration 0.5 hour
Maximum elevation 1150 m
Elevation gain 80 m
Map 92 P/6 Green Lake
GPS N51.26 W 121.04

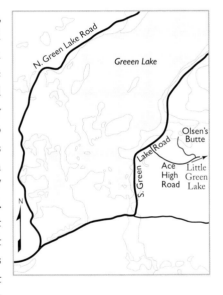

Access: From 100 Mile House, drive south on Highway 24 and take Watch Lake Road to North Green Lake Road. Continue east to the end of the paved road and 1 km farther along a bumpy dirt road past Ace High Road to a T-junction where three trails diverge in a meadow. The one on the right is signed Green Lake/Pressy Lake Forestry Road. The middle one continues east through the meadow. The left trail is the access road to Olsen's Butte. Park here if you do not have a high-centred vehicle, or farther up at the cattle guard if you do. Snowmobile trail #10, left of the cattleguard, is the trail to the summit.

Olsen's Butte is an outstanding location from which to view Green Lake and the Marble Mountains beyond, but since the short walk hardly justifies the long drive, consider exploring some of the other trails in the vicinity, such as the meadow trail and the short trail to Little Green Lake, a great picnic spot. The latter trail begins at the T-junction and swings right through the meadow for 500 m.

17. CRATER LAKE

Easy trails
Distance 2 km (combined)
Duration 0.5 hour
Map 92 P/6 Green Lake

Access: Highway 97 to 70 Mile House and east 25 km on North Bonaparte Road. The road is paved to begin with then becomes a good-quality gravel road. The entrance to Crater Lake is hard to spot. At around 24 km, watch for the yellow road marker sign 3239. The entrance is 500 m past this on the right indicated by a tiny snowmobile trail sign. Park just off the road.

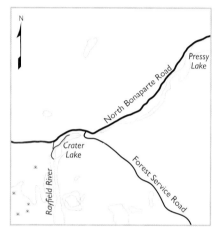

If Crater Lake were located near a larger population centre, it would surely rate as one of that area's top visitor attractions. As it is, this scenic gem remains one of the Cariboo's best-kept secrets. Despite its name, the lake does not owe its origins to a wayward meteor. Culver Canyon, through which the Rayfield River plunges to the lake, and the layers of basaltic rock, are linked to the same dynamic chain of events that created Painted Chasm. From the parking spot it is only a short walk to the canyon rim. A trail to the left heads down to Culver Canyon and the river, continuing along the bank to a spot near the highway – about 1 km in all. At low water, you can cross the river and work your way up to the rim on the south side of the canyon for more dramatic views. To the right of the canyon rim on the north side, another trail leads down to the bowl but no farther.

Crater Lake from the east rim.

Ted Newbery on the east rim, Crater Lake.

Canim Lake/Mahood Lake Area

Canim Lake is a stunningly beautiful 40-km-long body of water located 37 km east of 100 Mile House. It is a popular fishing and recreation destination well-served with resorts and a lakeside provincial campground.

The south road around Canim Lake leads to Mahood Lake, 25 km long, at the southwest border of Wells Gray Park. Strictly speaking, the lake and some of the hikes described here lie outside the boundaries of the Cariboo, but only just. I have included Mahood in this guide because it makes such a great base from which to explore this very attractive area nibbling at the Cariboo's eastern fringe.

Not quite Everest! Hiking party atop Big Timothy Mountain.

Looking toward the Deceptions, Big Timothy Mountain.

18. BIG TIMOTHY MOUNTAIN

Easy/moderate hike
Distance 7 km
Duration 2.5 hours
Maximum elevation 2155 m
Elevation gain 600 m
Map 93 A/2 McKinley Creek

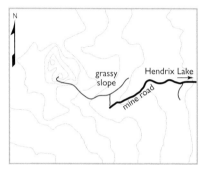

Access: Highway 97 from 100 Mile House to the Forest Grove turnoff. At the Forest Grove store, turn right onto Canim Lake Road. Where the road forks, keep straight around the north side of Canim Lake. The hardtop soon gives way to gravel/dirt. Stay on this road all the way to Hendrix Lake, 60 km from 100 Mile House. Look for the mining road on the left just past the road (right) to the Hendrix Lake townsite. Drive uphill 10 km to the rock barrier and the warning sign. Park here.

There are two mountains in the Cariboo with similar names: Mount Timothy near Lac la Hache and Big Timothy Mountain, featured here. Theories as to the origin of the name differ. One ties it to the wild timothy grass, while another has it a corruption of the Shuswap name Takomkane. Whatever the source of its name, Big Timothy certainly yields big views. From the saddle, there are glorious vistas of Boss and Deception Mountains and the peaks of Wells Gray Park. Beyond the saddle awaits some gentle walking around a series of tarns to a larger pond at the end of the alpine meadow. Big Timothy itself is a treeless volcanic cinder cone rising out of the meadow like an upturned cornet. The window of opportunity for hiking the mountain is short. Late August or September, when the pesky flies have subsided, are probably the most pleasant times to hike there. We've been blizzarded out in June and eaten alive in July, but we were compensated somewhat in the latter month by the display of wildflowers.

To reach the open pit molybdenum mine site from the barrier, continue uphill on the road and head right at the first intersection, about 400 m along. After 1 km, another road intersects on the left. Ignore it

The volcanic cone of Big Timothy provides the background for a great day's hiking.

Glacial tarn, Big Timothy area.

Returning from Big Timothy Mountain.

and stay right, heading across the excavation – the flat, rock-strewn area – toward the trees. You will notice a grassy east-facing slope above the area you are headed toward. Cross the redirected stream (obviously channelled) and head up and to the right until you locate an old Cat (as in machinery) track. Go left as you intersect this track and it should lead you to an obvious trail of spongy pine needles. The first section, and parts in between before you reach the saddle, can involve a bit of searching. The route is marked only by the occasional ribbon of survey tape, and tends to become overgrown from lack of regular use. Keep the notch or saddle in mind as your target and work your way toward it.

Hendrix Lake Townsite

Having driven this far, it is worthwhile taking time to visit the former mining community on the shores of Hendrix Lake. Built in 1964 by the Noranda Exploration Company to house some 250 workers of the Boss Mountain molybdenum mine, the community once boasted a three-room school, curling rink, tennis courts and a recreation hall. The mine was active until 1983 when it closed permanently. Since then some of the homes have been purchased and moved to other communities, and a number are still used as summer cottages. The foundations of the original mine offices and additional accommodation for workers can be seen on the walk from the mine road barrier to the open pit mine site.

The Canim River rushes toward Mahood Lake.

A quiet stretch of the Canim River.

Mahood Lake Campground

Access: Highway 97 from 100 Mile House to the Forest Grove turnoff. At the Forest Grove store, turn right onto Canim Lake Road. Where this road branches, take the right fork around the south side of Canim Lake and continue all the way to Wells Gray Park

The campground at Mahood Lake is perhaps the most beautifully situated campground in the park. High mountain ridges border the 21-km lake, which sits among dense stands of ancient hemlock, cedar and cottonwood. The campground was once the site of an Aboriginal encampment and still yields the occasional spearhead from the days when the First Nations peoples speared whitefish at night by the light of torches dipped in pitch pots.

A first day's sightseeing from the campground might include the area's three spectacular waterfalls and a short hike along the Canim River trail. This adds up to a very gentle itinerary, as two of the falls are only short walk-ins from the road.

Behind the Name Mahood

James Adam Mahood headed one of three Canadian Pacific survey parties in the 1870s searching for a route for the CPR through the "sea of mountains" to the Pacific. After much gruelling exploration in wild terrain, Mahood submitted his proposal for a route from Clearwater Lake to the coast via Mahood Lake, Canim Lake, Lac la Hache, Soda Creek, across the Chilcotin Plateau and south to Butte Inlet. The ten years of tough surveying by Mahood and crews headed by Sandford Fleming and others went for naught when the CPR announced its choice of the Kicking Horse Pass route in 1881.

19. MAHOOD FALLS AND CANIM FALLS

Easy hike
Distance 1 to 2 km
Durations 0.2 hour Mahood; 0.5 hour Canim
Map 92 P/15 Canim Lake

Access: The trailhead for both falls is indicated by a sign on the left-hand side of the road 6 km before the Mahood Lake campground. There is a parking pull-in on the right.

The two waterfalls located between Canim and Mahood

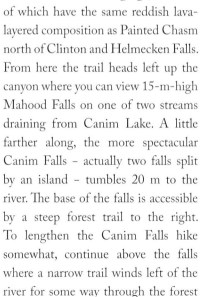

lakes are worth visiting even though there is not a lot of hiking involved. An 800-m walk brings you to the rim of the Canim River gorge, the walls

Canim Falls.

of which have the same reddish lava-layered composition as Painted Chasm north of Clinton and Helmecken Falls. From here the trail heads left up the canyon where you can view 15-m-high Mahood Falls on one of two streams draining from Canim Lake. A little farther along, the more spectacular Canim Falls – actually two falls split by an island – tumbles 20 m to the river. The base of the falls is accessible by a steep forest trail to the right. To lengthen the Canim Falls hike somewhat, continue above the falls where a narrow trail winds left of the river for some way through the forest before petering out.

55

20. *CANIM RIVER TRAIL*

Easy hike
Distance 2 km
Duration 0.75 hour
Map 92 P/15 Canim Lake

Access: The trailhead is located just under 1 km past the Mahood Lake campground. Watch for a clearing on the left past the park service road. Park here and walk in. The trail is signed as 0.5 km but actually continues farther.

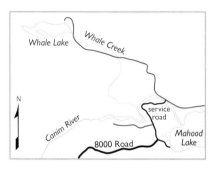

At one time, it was possible to hike this trail upstream 6 km to the Canim River Falls. Today it is only possible to safely hike a little over 2 km before encountering snags

caused by blowdown and areas where the river, in high runoff years, has cut away the banks. It is a pleasant walk nevertheless, made even more worthwhile by encountering the substantial remains of the old Scott family homestead, circa 1907, located on the riverbank and some tumbledown outbuildings on the left. Determined hikers, willing to clamber over downed trees and negotiate the narrow trail from the 2 km mark, are rewarded with lovely views of the Canim River as it rushes toward Mahood Lake.

On the Canim River trail.

21. WHALE LAKE TRAIL

Easy hike
Distance 5 km
Duration 1.5 hours
Maximum elevation 950 m
Elevation gain 300 m
Map 92 P/15 Canim Lake

Access: Right of the Mahood Lake campground entrance and across the Canim River bridge. The traihead is on the left immediately after the bridge.

An attractive hike to a secluded mountain lake through aspen and birch forest in the lower reaches.

For the first 400 m, the trail follows alongside the Canim River before swinging northward into the forest of mainly aspen and birch with increasing fir and cedar higher up. About one hour into the hike the trail begins to descend through a fairly tangled section with many sizeable deadfalls requiring some detouring around. The forest becomes quite dense as you near the picturesque aquamarine lake. Once there, there is little opportunity to hike farther. The trail comes to an abrupt end at a little beach. Beyond this point the forest is so thick and tangled it is pretty well impassable.

Hiking to Whale Lake.

22. *DECEPTION FALLS TRAIL*

Easy hike

Distance I km to viewpoint, 2 km to rim

Duration 0.5 hour

Maximum elevation 760 m

Elevation gain 165 m

Maps 92 P/15 Canim Lake and 92 P/16 Mahood Lake

Access: From the Wells Gray Park entrance, head right. Just after it crosses the Canim River Bridge the road narrows to a bumpy single-lane track proceeding uphill for 4 km above the north shore of Mahood Lake. The Deception Falls trailhead is indicated by a tiny sign on the left.

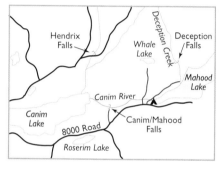

It is a short and pleasant walk to the falls through aspen and birch forest carpeted in salmonberry. The trail is well-maintained but suffers blowdowns that tend to clutter the path in places until the ranger and his saw can get to them. The best time to hike here is the autumn, when the aspen are a sea of yellow. The falls is a glorious 40-m plunge down a narrow gorge. The trail left snakes alongside the safety fence and up to the rim, providing superb

Through aspen forest en route to Deception Falls.

views of the cascade. On the right is a steep descent into the gorge where Deception Creek rushes toward Mahood Lake. To lengthen the hike, a narrow trail on the left heads uphill through the forest for a kilometre or so, gradually narrowing to a game trail.

Behind the Name Deception

A surveying error rather than an outright deception is what earned the creek its name. In 1873, CPR surveyor E.W. Jarvis, mistook this creek for the Clearwater River he had been instructed to explore. Although Jarvis later recognized his mistake, another CPR surveyor, Joseph Hunter, retracing Jarvis's route, was not amused at having wasted time thrashing needlessly about in the bush. His choice of name reflects his displeasure.

Deception Falls plunges 40 m along Deception Creek.

100 Mile House

The municipality of 100 Mile House, located midway between Clinton and Williams Lake, is the commercial hub of the region extending from Lac la Hache in the north to Bridge Lake in the east. Within its radius are a number of smaller communities that, added to 100 Mile's 1,900 souls, brings the total area population to around 22,000 and growing. The lumber industry, including a thriving log-home-building sector, along with ranching and tourism form the economic mainstays of the area.

The lovely rolling terrain in and around 100 Mile House makes for great hiking, biking and horseback riding, as well as cross-country skiing. The area trails are especially suitable for family recreation. There is nothing forbidding here – a few small hills only, and miles of meadow ranchland interspersed with creeks, ponds and lakes. Just north of 100 Mile House, the 108 Ranch community offers more of the same, plus a superb network of cross-country ski trails.

Historical Background

100 Mile House originally was known as Bridge Creek House when Thomas Miller owned the ramshackle collection of buildings catering to the traffic of the fur trade. Construction of the actual roadhouse began in 1862 to serve the needs of those journeying to and from the goldfields. With the building of the Cariboo Wagon Road, Bridge Creek House, located 100 Miles from Lillooet, became the 100 Mile House.

Along with this increased activity came the need to provide food for the travellers, thus leading to the development of the ranching business in the area with herds being driven north from the United States.

In 1930 an unlikely immigrant, Lord Martin Cecil, left England to come to 100 Mile House to manage the estate owned by his father, the Marquis of Exeter. At that time the population numbered 12, and the only buildings were the original roadhouse, a general store, a post office, a telegraph office and a power plant. In 1937 the old roadhouse, like so many wooden buildings along the Cariboo Road, burned to the ground.

The original 100 Mile House Ranch has since been split up: the section west of the highway is operated by Bridge Creek Ranch, while the 100 Mile Ranch lies east of the road. The Bridge Creek barn has been relocated to the meadow within the 100 Mile Ranch corrals. A relic of the gold rush days, a fully restored Concord coach, pride of the BX Stagelines, is on display outside the Red Coach Inn.

Bridge Creek twists and turns on its way to Horse Lake.

23. *100 MILE WILDLIFE MARSH TRAIL*

Easy stroll

Distance 1.5 km

Duration 0.5 hour

Map 92 P/11 100 Mile House

Access: The visitor information centre adjacent to Highway 97.

In 1974, at a time when most BC communities were filling in their marshes, the 100 Mile Naturalists, the Rotary Club and village council were attempting to protect theirs. Their efforts paid off the following year when the marsh was designated a wildlife sanctuary, and Ducks Unlimited and Fish and Wildlife lent their expertise to the project. The result is one of only a few such refuges to be found in the middle of a municipality.

To begin, walk to the right of the information centre, along the shore and around the west end of the marsh and across the bridge. From there the trail meanders below the high school and back to the starting point. In the early summer, large families of yellow goslings can be seen feeding by the road, while the red-headed and yellow-headed blackbirds noisily establish territory from atop the bullrushes around the pond.

24. *CENTENNIAL PARK TRAILS*

Easy hikes
Distance 1 to 3 km
Duration 0.5 to 1 hour
Map 92 P/11 100 Mile House

Access: Centennial Park. Enter from Cedar Avenue, between the daycare building and the Parkside Centre, downhill to the parking area.

From the parking lot, trails head north, south and east. The prettiest little walk is to the Bridge Creek Falls, about 1 km alongside the creek to the falls and beyond to the campground on Horse Lake Road. At the bottom of the falls, a rusting chimney structure is all that

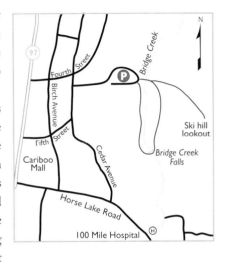

remains of an old water-powered sawmill. The falls are an attractive sight anytime, but winter offers the most dramatic scenes when the frozen spray creates spectacular ice art.

To the left of the parking lot another attractive walk leads north past the tennis courts and, with the creek on the right, to the bottom of Evergreen Crescent and the start of the Willowdale trails. About halfway along on the right a bridge provides access to more walks on the east side. Additional trails are found by crossing the bridge by the parking lot. One of these heads to the base of the ski hill, while a turnoff to the left about halfway to the hill provides access to the Willowdale area from that side.

25. *100 MILE DEMONSTRATION FOREST TRAIL*

Easy hike

Distance 7-km loop

Duration 1.5 hours

Maximum elevation 1190 m

Elevation gain 125 m

Map 92 P/11 100 Mile House

Access: From 100 Mile, drive 3 km south on Highway 97. The access road is on the right just after the bridge and is signed 99 Mile Nordic Ski Trails and Snowmobile Club trails. The demonstration forest is 1 km along on the right and is signed.

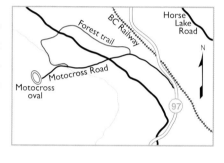

While the primary purpose of a demonstration forest is, of course, education, if you can combine this with an attractive walk, then it's not a bad way to spend a few hours in the outdoors. With the exception of the final stretch, which is on a dirt road, this particular walk is quite pleasurable and always informative. At a couple of points along the way, there are detours to view displays of old forestry equipment and machinery.

Separate from the demonstration forest, but starting right at the entrance to it, forestry workers have cleared brush and trees from a 1.2-km section of the Cariboo Wagon Road that winds through the forest to the railway tracks by the highway. A notice board details the history of the old artery, and you can clearly see the ruts created by the passing wagons and stagecoaches all those years ago.

A detailed brochure on the demonstration forest can be obtained from the 100 Mile visitor information centre, and guided tours of the forest can be arranged if you'd like more information than is provided.

26. *SKI HILL TRAIL*

Easy/moderate hike
Distance 2 km
Duration 1 hour
Maximum elevation 1115 m
Elevation gain 200 m
Map 92 P/11 100 Mile House

Access: Centennial Park. From the parking lot, cross the bridge and head uphill. At 0.5 km you will encounter a fence. Go through under the power lines. The road resumes on the other side. Continue to the base of the ski hill, where you have a choice of three paths to the summit. The first one is the least attractive and the most demanding. The farthest one is the longest but easiest, and the middle one is slightly shorter. Return on either one.

The former ski hill is the highest point in the immediate area and provides great views of 100 Mile and Timothy Mountain to the north, the Exeter valley to the west and the Willowdale area to the northeast. In the 1970s this was 100 Mile's ski hill, until a lack of snow forced its closure after only a few years of operation. A successful downhill facility has since been established at Mount Timothy, east of Lac la Hache.

From the ski hill, looking north to Stephenson Lake.

27. HORSE LAKE RIDGE

Easy/moderate hike
Distance 4. 5 km
Duration 1.25 hours
Max elevation 1135 m
Elevation gain 220 m
Map 92/P11 100 Mile House

Access: See Ski Hill hike #26.

Horse Lake Ridge runs east from the old ski hill, above Horse Lake Road and Horse Lake itself. It is accessible from various points between 100 Mile and the Imperial Ranchettes subdivision at Horse Lake. The climb to the top of the ski hill is steep, but once you're on the ridge it is easy walking to a lookout point, a clearing about 2.5 km along, with its fine views of the Marble Mountains to the southwest and southeast to Lone Butte.

The lookout point from Horse Lake Ridge.

28. HORSE LAKE LOOKOUT

Easy hike
Distance 6 km
Duration 1.5 hours
Maximum elevation 1185 m
Elevation gain 200 m
Map 92 P/11 100 Mile House

Access: From Highway 97, take Horse Lake Road to the Imperial Ranchettes subdivision and proceed to the end of Lakeshore Drive. The trail begins at the road's end.

A pleasant meadow and forest walk affording great views of Horse Lake and beyond, the trail is easy for the most part, with one steep uphill and downhill section. Osprey and bald eagles are commonly sighted above the lake and perched in trees along the shoreline.

At the start gate, take the trail, right, overlooking the lake. After 1 km, the trail swings left uphill through the forest (the trail on the right continues only a short way above the lake, ending at a fence line). At 2.5 km, the trail meets a gravel road running west to east. Heading to the right, about 40 m along this road pick up the trail again on the left. Keep left all the way to the lookout – a grassy clearing on the ridge top. From the lookout, the return half of the route continues sharply downhill to a clearing and a dirt road. Head left from here and turn left again on the gravel road you crossed on the way up. About 60 m along, note the gate in the fence on your right by an old gravel pit. Cross here and take the trail on the left as you enter the woods. Continue downhill to rejoin the trail back to the start.

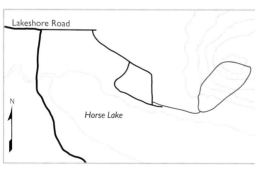

29a. *LITTLE BRIDGE CREEK FALLS*

Easy hike
Distance 0.6 km
Duration 0.15 hour
Map 92 P/11 100 Mile House

Access: There are two ways to access the Doug MacLeod Trail to Little Bridge Creek Falls. One requires just a short walk through the woods to a pleasant picnic spot. The other, for those with some mountain-biking experience, involves a much longer route from 99 Mile via the cross-country ski trails.

Via Exeter Road and 1100 road, drive 14 km to the 800 road on the left. Cross the cattle guard and park on the right. The sign for the Doug Macleod Trail is on the opposite side of the road, to the right of the stream.

Little Bridge Creek, Exeter Meadows.

29b. *CARIBOO MARATHON ROUTE*

Intermediate/advanced mountain bike
Distance 20 km
Duration 4.5 hours
Maximum elevation 1188 m
Elevation gain/loss 40 m
Map 99 Mile Ski trails map
GPS N 51.37 W 121.25

Access: From the 99 Mile Nordics ski lodge, follow the Cariboo Marathon Route in reverse to the west checkpoint. The checkpoint is on the left at a clearing about 10 km out, following a long downhill section, and is indicated by a yellow ski trail sign. The lettering, however, is on the reverse side of the sign, facing away from you. Across the clearing is a short connecting road to the 800 forestry road. Turn right and downhill 1 km. Park just before the cattle guard. On the right, note the Peter Skene Woodlot sign and, to the left of this, a sign indicating the Doug MacLeod Trail. On the return, go back to the marathon route and north and east to the day lodge.

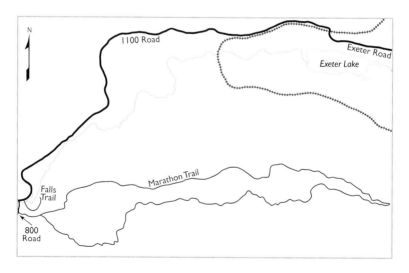

30. *MUSHER'S BRIDGE TRAIL*

Easy hike
Distance 7.5-km loop
Duration 2 hours
Map 92 P/11

Access: See Ski Hill Trail, hike #26. From the parking lot, Centennial Park, cross the bridge onto the ski hill approach road. Just after the hydro corridor watch for a trail on the left signed "Bridge Creek Trails."

Some years ago, dog team drivers held dogsled races in Willowdale and crossed this

bridge en route, hence the name. This is a lovely walk, combining forest and meadowland, with Bridge Creek winding alongside on the return leg and great views from the sandy cliffs overlooking the creek as it coils its way east in a series of oxbows. There is muskrat and beaver activity along the watershed and a variety of wildfowl, as well as great blue heron and kingfisher. Deer and coyote also frequent the area.

The first leg of the trail, actually a dirt road, makes a curve through a meadow with the ski hill on the right

Musher's Bridge, Willowdale.

before straightening out and heading eastward through the forest. On a downhill stretch, watch for a trail turning off left. Turn onto this and continue downhill through the forest to the bridge. On the other side, the trail climbs uphill for the return portion of the loop. Go left here, and, rather than walk the dirt road, follow the track along the bluffs above the creek for as long as you can before having to rejoin the dirt road. It is a much more attractive walk this way. Continue on the dirt road to Little Bridge Creek and the fence line of 100 Mile Ranch. Here the trail swings south alongside the back fences of homes on Evergreen Crescent. A short way along, Bridge Creek emerges on the left and the trail leads directly into Centennial Park.

Bridge Creek from Musher's Bridge.

31. *WILLOWDALE CABIN*

Easy hike, bike
Distance 9.5-km loop
Duration 2.5 hours
Map 92 P/11 100 Mile House

Access: Centennial Park.

This route basically extends the Musher's Bridge loop to provide a longer hike. Our destination is a cabin once used by skiers in the 1970s when there were groomed cross-country trails through Willowdale.

For the outward leg, we follow the previous hike in reverse, heading left from the parking lot through the park and alongside the back gardens of the homes and across Little Bridge Creek. From here we swing right along Willowdale, again, choosing the paths on the right along the river bluffs wherever possible for the best views. Continue along the bluffs until it becomes necessary to rejoin the dirt road that leads down to a bridge, on the other side of which the cabin is located. For the return leg, just after you crossed the bridge on the approach, you would have noticed a trail on the right. This is your route. The trail heads into the woods a short way before entering a meadow. Cross the fence and stay on this clearly defined ranching/logging road until you intersect the ski hill road, where you turn right and continue across the power line corridor to Centennial Park.

Bridge Creek Oxbow, Willowdale.

The 108 Mile Area

With its more than 100 km of fine ski trails, the 108 Mile area is widely recognized as a premier cross-country ski destination. For the remainder of the year, the 26,000 acres comprising the 108 Ranch community, with its areas of greenbelt and adjacent ranchlands, becomes the domain of the hiker, mountain biker and horseback rider, who relishes the tranquil beauty of its long stretches of meadowland dotted with ponds and teeming with wildfowl. Located on the western edge of the Pacific Migratory Flyway, this is a great place to view bird life, including exotics, such as the sandhill crane, and many raptors: bald eagles, osprey, assorted hawks. Mammals common to the area include muskrat, fox, coyote, mule deer and black bear.

The 108 Heritage Site

The 108 Mile area is inseparable from its history, and where better to view the past than at the restored buildings at the South Cariboo Heritage Site, located just off Highway 97 at the 108 Ranch north entrance. The site encapsulates the history of the area in seven picturesque acres. Located on the grounds are some of the refurbished log buildings of the original 108 Stopping House, constructed in the 1860s. The stately 105 Mile Ranch house, dating back to 1909, was moved to its present location in 1979 and serves as a museum. Most striking of all is the massive barn erected in 1908 by Captain Lionel Watson to house his one hundred imported Clydesdale horses. The restoration work involved in saving this structure is a story in itself. In recent years a historic logging exhibit has been added to the site, as well as a log chapel with original furnishings. Discussions are in progress to lease an adjoining acreage for the creation of a cultural centre to present the history and culture of the Northern Secwepemc (Shuswap) First Nations.

The 108 Recreational Ranch

The heart of the 108 Mile area is this unique development 15 km north of 100 Mile House. It was originally conceived by Block Bros. Realty, which purchased the 105 and 108 Mile Ranch properties in 1968 as a cottage community to appeal to southerners who would fly in, relax and enjoy the tranquility of the area. Instead, those who came tended to fall in love with the place and put down roots.

The original concept, which envisioned only 3,000 of the entire 26,000 acres developed and the remainder left untouched as common land, was a remarkable one, given that concern for the environment was not a priority in those days. "In Partnership With Nature" was the marketing slogan employed to sell the hundreds of half- to one-acre lots, and it was an honest pitch. The 108 was designed to be a total recreational enterprise, with trails for hiking, skiing and riding, and lakes for swimming, canoeing and fishing. As a further enticement, a 5,000-ft. aircraft runway was constructed, along with a resort hotel and golf course.

Today, the 108 Recreational Ranch is a community of more than 3,000, many of whom work in 100 Mile House. Block Bros. is no more. Of the original 23,000 undeveloped acres, some were sold back to the Monical family, who operate the 105 Mile Ranch and retain grazing rights in Walker Valley and elsewhere. Another parcel became The Hills Health & Guest Ranch. Thanks to the efforts of an enlightened Property Owners Association, now the Ranch Community Association, thousands of acres of the original parcel remain common land designated as greenbelt, and rights-of-way have been granted through some of the remainder.

Opposite::
(Top left) Pete Kitchen Lake.
(Top right) Rolling ranchlands, Pete Kitchen Lake.
(Mid left) Old trapper's cabin, 108 Heritage Site.
(Mid right) Overlooking Pete Kitchen Lake.
(Bottom) 108 Mile Lake from the lookout.

32. *108/SEPA LAKE TRAILS*

Easy hikes
Distance 9.5 km combined
Duration 2.4 hours
Map 92 P/11 100 Mile House

Access: From the 108 Heritage Site, walk to the bridge over Sucker Creek and go left.

An attractive walk around the two lakes, which have a wide littoral zone teeming with bird life in the spring and early summer. Yellow- and red-headed blackbirds compete noisily for territory among the bullrushes in spring, and the

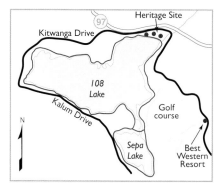

lakes are home to a rich variety of wildfowl including Canada geese, coots, buffleheads, mergansers, grebes and several loon families. Osprey and bald eagles patrol 108 Lake for its stocked rainbows and resident course fish. The eagles are frequently seen dive-bombing the baby ducks and loons.

From the bridge, the trail winds around the lake, past the main beach, below the golf course to Sepa Lake. Sepa Lake and 108 Lake used to be joined by a channel, but in recent years this channel has dried up, isolating Sepa Lake. At Sepa Lake you make the choice to limit the walk to just 108 Lake, continue right around Sepa Lake and return to the starting point, to take in both lakes. On the north side of 108 Lake, the trail crosses a pair of bridges with lagoons on the left that, sadly, have also been drying up in recent years and could well be nothing but dried mud and vegetation by now.

33. *108 LOOKOUT LOOP*

Easy hike

Distance 6 km

Duration 1.5 hours

Maximum elevation 1005 m

Elevation gain 115 m

Map 92 P/11 100 Mile House

Access: From the parking lot across from the 108 Heritage Site, walk south to the Highway 97 underpass. The tunnel provides access to trails on the east side of the 108

The hike to the lookout is a popular one and can be done as either up and back or a loop. The loop provides more variety and also the opportunity to design your own return leg by opting for a different combination of trails as shown on the cross-country ski map boards located along the way. From the top, there are fine views of 108 Lake to the west and Sucker Lake to the southeast.

For this loop, exit the tunnel on the east side of the highway, cross the cattle guard and head right along the road until you spot ski trail #2 on the left. Walk up trail #2, to the intersection with trail #3 (about 2 km to this point). Remain on trail #2 watching for a path on the left about 400 m along. This is the path to the lookout. On top, the trail skirts along the cliff edge then downhill on the north side of the bluff. At the bottom, keep left on the wider trail, which soon meets up with trail #3. This will take you to the intersection of trails #2 and #3 again. From here follow #2 back to the tunnel.

34. *SUCKER LAKE TRAIL*

Easy hike, bike
Distance 8.5-km loop
Duration 2 hours
Maximum elevation 945 m
Elevation gain 30 m
Maps 92 P/11 100 Mile House and 92 P/14 Lac la Hache

Access: From the underpass across from the 108 Heritage Site, turn left to meet the road running uphill.

This well-established trail has long been popular with joggers, walkers and horseback riders for its variety of meadow, forest and lake scenery. The first part of the route, uphill to Sucker Lake, is on the old 108 stagecoach road that went all the way past Sucker Lake to Horsefly in the 1860s. At Sucker Lake our trail swings right along the east shore then around the south end of the lake, crossing a Ducks Unlimited water control outlet and into open meadow. The final stretch is through grazing lands punctuated with stands of trembling aspen. It is a pleasant hike at any time of the year.

Sucker Lake.

35. SODA LAKE

Easy hike, bike
Distance 6 km
Duration 1.25-hour hike
Maps 92 P/14 Lac la Hache

Access: See Sucker Lake Trail, hike #34

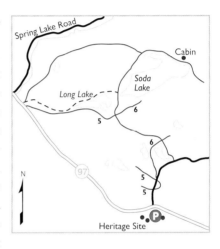

Our destination is the crumbling rancher's shelter on the east shore of Soda Lake. The lake itself is fairly shallow, alkaline and not all that attractive, but the surroundings are quite beautiful. While this is ranchland and fraught with cows, there is a surprising variety of wildlife. There must be food of some sort in the lake that it doesn't deter the duck population, and nearby (freshwater) ponds support large numbers of Canada geese. The unmistakable, primitive-sounding croak of sandhill cranes is often heard as you near the cabin, their sensitive hearing detecting intruders a long way off. While the number of eastern bluebirds appears to fluctuate from year to year, they seem to favour the aspen stands at the south end of the lake. Coyote and fox are around and black bear, too, in the less open areas

The road to Soda Lake is located on the left about 1.5 km up Sucker Lake Road from the underpass. A road sign by the highway identifies this as Hickling Road, but it is commonly referred to by the former name and that is how it will be identified for all hikes in this area. There is no sign to indicate Soda Lake Road, but the intersection appears on the left following a relatively flat stretch of the approach road and just before the road starts to climb. From this point there is only one intersection along the way where ski trails #5 and #6 meet. Continue across and downhill through the woods. As you exit this wooded segment, the lake will appear on your right. From here follow the road uphill and to the right at the top of the rise. The cabin should be visible at the east end of the lake.

On the return, for variety's sake, there is an interesting little detour that can pay dividends in wildlife viewing and photography opportunities, while not adding any distance to the walk. About 500 m before Soda Lake Road intersects Sucker Lake Road (GPS reading N 51.45 W 121.20), you might notice a pond on the left screened by trees. An old ski trail, #6, heads off to the right and makes a circle around and behind the pond to meet Sucker Lake Road farther down. As you make the turn around this pond, look downhill to the right and you will find a secluded little lake set among the trees.

Approaching Soda Lake.

36. LONG LAKE LOOP

Easy hike
Distance 10.5-km loop
Duration 2.5 hours
Map 92/ P 11 100 Mile House

Access: Via the tunnel at the 108 rest stop, turn left to meet Sucker Lake Road (Hickling Road) and turn right. A few metres along, notice a track on the left heading uphill north.

There are so many trails and old logging roads east of Highway 97 in the 108 Mile area that practically any combination will provide a good hike. This particular loop has an especially attractive section where it winds around a long peanut-shaped pond filled with the usual assortment of wildfowl. There are views of the wooded hills to the east of Soda Lake, and a little clambering up the hillsides by the pond enables a long look back down the valley to the cattle pens and sagging log buildings of 111 Mile.

From Sucker Lake Road, the trail climbs for 1.5 km before dropping down toward 111 Mile. The bottom of the hill, 3.5 km from the start, marks the top of the loop. At the bottom of the hill, turn right, ignoring the wider trail through the woods, and locate what amounts to a cow path skirting the edge of the trees until it intersects a cattle path heading uphill eastward close to the edge of the forest. The path cuts through a small gully and continues through the meadow down and around the north side of Long Lake (more of a pond than a lake) until it meets Soda Lake Road. Turn right at this point and follow the directions for the return portion of the previous hike, Soda Lake Trail #35.

Thunder clouds building over Long Lake.

37. *111 MILE CREEK*

Easy hike/bike
Distance 7 km
Duration 1.5-hour hike
Map 92 P/14 Lac la Hache

Access: See Soda Lake, hike #35.

The 111 Mile Creek area is a very attractive location in itself and is easily reached by car via Spring Lake Road, 7 km north of 108 Mile House. There are lovely walks along either side of the stream east or west, but those looking for a full day hike or a good mountain-biking trip might prefer this more challenging route.

Follow the directions for Soda Lake, but before turning right at the top of the rise to head to the cabin, note two trails on the left. You want the second of those. Following a forested section, the trail winds steeply down toward the creek paralleling Spring Lake Road. Locating the stream crossing takes a bit of searching, but once you are on the level section at the bottom of the hill, watch for a depression where the original bridge was located. A few metres past this, watch for a narrow

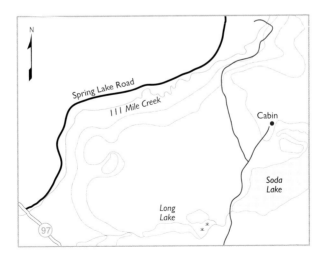

Heading downhill to 111 Mile Creek.

trail in the bushes that leads down to a makeshift bridge. If you fail to locate this, cross where you can. On the other side is an open area that sometimes functions as a parking spot. From here you can investigate paths right or left along the creek.

38. *PETE KITCHEN LAKE*

Easy hike
Distance 3.5 km
Duration I hour
Elevation gain 100 m
Map 92 P/14 Lac la Hache

Access: Highway 97 to Spring Lake Road. Drive 3 km and park on the right in the open area by the stream.

More meadows, more ponds. This time a bit higher up, permitting wonderful views of the 111 Mile Creek area southward. The land hereabouts is part of the 105 Mile Ranch holdings, and care should be taken to avoid spooking cattle. Sandhill cranes return to this area each spring to nest, and you may hear their alarmed din as you approach.

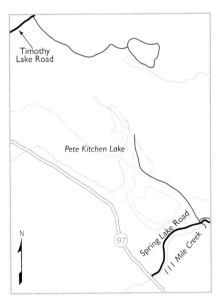

From the parking area, cross the road and look for a cattle path running alongside the road. Head left and walk about 300 m then cut uphill and over the crest. The trail runs through the middle of the meadow and passes a number of ponds on the left before heading downhill to Pete Kitchen Lake on the right. To see more of the area, head counter-clockwise around the lake and enjoy the gently rolling terrain on the north side.

39. *EXPRESS MEADOWS*

Easy hike, bike
Distance 12-km loop
Duration 3 hour hike
Map 92 P/11 100 Mile House

Access: Via the tunnel at the 108 rest stop, cross the cattle guard and head right to Sucker Lake. At the point where the trail curves north, to go around the lake, note a trail on the right passing a small pond. The pond, however, has been evaporating of late and could possibly have dried up altogether.

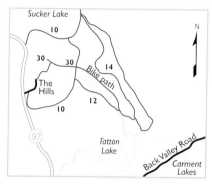

This is another of these quintessentially peaceful Cariboo hikes combining a lake and beautiful long meadows liberally sprinkled with ponds. Express Meadows owes its name to the BC Express Company, whose stage and wagon horses were once pastured here.

From the pond, the trail swings to the right into Express Meadows, and from there a number of trails head down to the ponds at the end. Once there, if the grassy area at the head of the pond is dry enough, it is possible to walk or bike around to the west side. Otherwise, you may have to take the trail left through the woods to the power line and right. At the top of a rise on the west side just above the meadows, look for ski trail #14, which runs through the woods. Continue on this for a while before cutting right, into the meadow and back the way you entered.

Express Meadows, west side.

40. *EXPRESS MEADOWS BIKE/SKI TRAILS COMBINATION*

Easy hike, bike
Distance 10-km loop
Duration 2-hour hike
Maps 108 Community Ski Trails map and 92 P/11 100 Mile House

Access: The 108 Hills Resort on Highway 97.

This slightly shorter route utilizes the 108 Hills ski trails and a single-track bicycle path to gain access to the same area described in hike #39.

From the 108 Hills head downhill to the left of the T-bar lift and right on trail #30 to the end, where it meets trail #10. Turn left and immediately encounter a fence across the trail designed to contain the Hills' horses. A walker's gate lets you through. Immediately on the right look for a narrow path heading off into the woods. The trail winds for less than 1 km before breaking out into the meadow. Continue along to the end and around the pond. After an uphill stretch, look for ski trail #12. Turn right here, crossing the ditch that exits the pond, and continue to the intersection with trail #10. Turn right on #10 to the intersection with trail #30 and back to the Hills.

Express Meadows, late fall.

Walker Valley Trails

Walker Valley is named after William Walker, who is listed in the documents at the 108 Heritage site as having operated the 108 Mile Roadhouse from 1880 to 1891. This beautiful stretch of ranchland, extending from the northern end of Watson Lake to the outskirts of Lac la Hache, falls into the category of "best kept secrets of the Cariboo." Known to few outside the immediate area, Walker Valley is a source of unending delight for those walkers and amateur naturalists familiar with its peaceful beauty.

The southern portion of the valley is designated greenbelt, and all of it is wildlife refuge and agricultural land reserve. Cattle belonging to the Monical family's 105 Mile Ranch graze the valley's bunchgrass, sharing the meadows with coyotes, fox and deer that keep mainly to the woods, as well as the odd black bear. In 1976 Ducks Unlimited started work on a project of constructing earthen control dams to create a chain of ponds along the valley's length, linked by the stream flowing out of Watson Lake. Following this, nesting islands were added to provide protection from predators. The results can be seen and enjoyed today, not only in the variety of duck life paddling the channels but also in spring when flocks of red-winged and yellow-headed blackbirds return to perch on the cattails, filling the air with their raucous din. The ponds are home also to beaver and muskrat, while raptors, such as marsh hawks, red-tailed hawks and the occasional bald eagle, make life interesting for the pond inhabitants. Swallows abound and western bluebirds are most often seen perched on fences along the edge of the ponds.

Name Origins – Watson Lake and Tatton Road

The name Watson is synonymous with the 108 Ranch, which has a lake, a creek, a former mansion and a massive horse barn named after Captain Geoffrey Lionel Watson of Britain's Yorkshire and Lancashire Regiment. Watson came to the Cariboo in 1904 and left in 1911. In between, he purchased the 50,000-acre Highland Ranch, built a giant 48 x 12 m barn, one of the largest in the country, to house one hundred purebred Clydesdale horses, and oversaw construction of a splendid mansion on present-day Tatton Road. Legend has it the home was built for a bride who never left England to settle in the Cariboo. On the other hand, the wealthy captain could well afford luxury and may simply have chosen to be comfortable. Watson eventually went to Europe to serve in the war and was killed in action, his estate passing to Lord Eggerton of Tatton, another English aristocrat, after whom Tatton Road is named.

Watson mansion eventually fell prey to vandals and souvenir hunters, who stripped away most of the furnishings and fittings, until a group bought the property and restored the house somewhat. Unfortunately, this shell of the once-great landmark burned to the ground in the early 1980s.

South end, Walker Valley.

41. *WALKER VALLEY SOUTH END LOOP*

Easy hike
Distance 5 km
Duration 1.25 hour
Map 92 P/11 100 Mile House

Access: Approaching from the south, turn left onto Tatton Road, 8 km north of 100 mile House. The entrance to Walker Valley is on the right, 3 km along Tatton Road at the north end of Watson Lake. Park on the short access road to the valley.

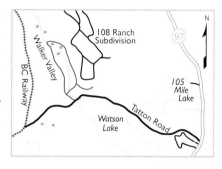

Binoculars and a good field guide for identifying ducks will add to the enjoyment of this gentle hike, which invites a lot of stopping to check out beaks. The work of Ducks Unlimited is much in evidence along the valley's length.

From the entrance gate, one path heads directly down the middle of the valley in the direction of the ponds, while another heads uphill. You can choose either, but the upper one is a woodland trail, while the other is through open meadow. Both are very pleasant routes. At the northern end of the ponds, the path swings right, crosses Watson Creek and continues by the eastern shore of the last pond. From here it climbs to a great viewpoint where you can look out over the valley south to Watson Lake. The trail heads downward from here, through a fence gate and along the hillside, with the ponds on the right and homes above on the left. As you approach Watson Lake, look for a path on the right leading down to the creek and back on the path you first came in on.

42. *WALKER VALLEY NORTH*

Easy hike, bike
Distance 4 km
Duration I hour
Maps 92 P/I I 100 Mile House and 92 P/I4 Lac la Hache

Access: From the 108's West Beach on Kitwanga Drive, park and walk north 400 m on Kalum Drive to where the gas pipeline meets the road. The access road to Walker Valley is on the right. Walk alongside the fence and enter the valley.

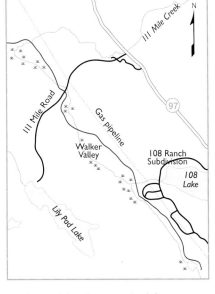

Our destination is the north end of the Walker Valley to the last pond in the chain. Detouring from the lower path now and then to the ridge above presents opportunities for out-standing views.

Once through the fence, head left downhill and pick up the valley trail heading north. After passing alongside a number of ponds, the path meets up with 111 Mile Road, which intersects on the right at the end of a pond. Continue curving left into the open meadow, with Watson Creek on the left. The trail continues to another, larger pond from which a creek exits eastward. Depending on how high the pond level is, you may have to wade across. From here, the path curves left around the head of this pond and crosses an earthen dam bordering another pond on the right. This marks the end of the valley. The area surrounding this last pond makes for attractive exploring and is a great picnic spot.

43. *GOOSE LAKE*

Easy bike
Distance 9 km
Duration 2 hours
Maps 92 P/11 100 Mile House and 92 P/14 Lac la Hache

Access: From the north entrance to Walker Valley on Kalum Drive.

This is an attractive, mainly meadows route with a little bit of pioneer history thrown in in the form of an old two-storey log ranch house located in the middle of a field. Because of the 18-km round-trip distance, the route is best tackled by mountain bike. Goose Lake itself is actually a large alkaline pond, home to a few ducks and sandpipers. A number of smaller ponds are located nearby, most of which dry up in the summer. The trip can be extended by heading right around the lake and locating a logging road on the right that continues all the way to Helena Lake. To venture this far, however, would require an overnight camp. For the walker, a hike as far as the old homestead would be about 7 km one way.

The first part of the route follows the Walker Valley North trail for 3.5 km until it intersects a road on the left. Turn onto this road and across the railway tracks. The trail to Goose Lake will be on the right about 1 km along. The entrance is a barbed-wire gate. From this point, continue

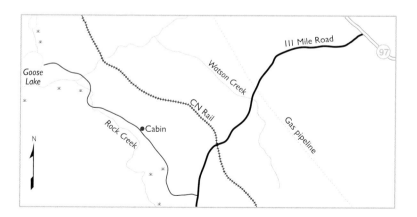

north until you come to an intersection. Take the right-hand trail that winds downhill through the forest. It's hard to spot, but there is a barely visible snowmobile trail sign, a white arrow on a tree on the right at this intersection, indicating the direction. From here it is 1.7 km to the old homestead in the meadow.

Continuing from the homestead, keep to the trail north through the meadow, ignoring any trails to the right. You may spot the occasional snowmobile arrow pointing the way. At 1.3 km from the cabin, the trail crosses dried-up Goose Creek. On the other side for a short way, the track narrows and hooks left before it widens again and continues through a wooded stretch to emerge at Goose Lake.

Old homestead, Goose Lake trail.

Refreshment stop, Goose Lake.

Wetlands, Walker Valley.

Walker Valley north.

Goose Lake photo op.

The Williams Lake Area

Williams Lake is more heavily forested and the recreational aspect less developed than the communities in the southern part of the region. Nevertheless, there are one or two good areas for hiking close in, and a number within easy reach of the city. Williams Lake is the gateway to the sparsely inhabited Chilcotin, which presents unlimited hiking opportunities.

Williams Lake – A Brief History

Settlement in the valley originally known by its Athapaskan name as Columneetza, "meeting of the princely ones," followed a familiar Cariboo pattern. The ancestors of the present-day Sugar Cane Band were living a semi-nomadic life here when the fur traders began filtering into the area from Fort Alexandria. Following the traders came the transient gold seekers and close on their heels arrived farmers and ranchers to pre-empt land in the valley. The city is thought to have acquired its present name around 1850 to honour the local Chief William, possibly a transliteration of his Shuswap name, Wesemaist.

With the Cariboo Wagon Road advancing north, the people of Williams Lake eagerly looked forward to its coming, expecting to reap the benefits as a trading centre. It was not to be, however, as the contractor elected to bypass the city and swing east at 150 Mile. As it turned out, Williams Lake survived rather nicely without "the road." The town had a stable economic base in grain growing, leading to the establishment of a flour mill and a brewery, and has diversified over the years into ranching, forestry and mining.

44. MISSION PONDS

Easy hike

Distance 3 km

Duration 0.75 hour

Map 93 A/4 150 Mile House

Access: Twenty km south of Williams Lake on the west side of the highway. Park on the shoulder.

There is something so captivating about this lovely stretch of rolling countryside with its cluster of kettle ponds and forested background that invites one to defy the barbed-wire cattle fences and go exploring. Some of the acreage to the southwest is privately owned and the Williams Lake Cattle Company either owns or leases a chunk. It is this section, from the ponds north and west to Cummings Lake, that merits exploring for its scenic beauty and amazing biodiversity. Here you will find cactus flowering in late June/early July. Several families of magpies have taken up residence. Usually magpies are found farther south and east beyond Cache Creek or west of the Fraser. There is a large concentration of red-tailed hawks, perhaps attracted by an abundance of ground squirrels. By the lake, common and spotted sandpipers skitter along the path, while lesser yellowlegs stilt along the shore. Deer tracks can be seen along the lakeshore, and coyotes den in the wooded copses near the ponds, while the ponds themselves are home to grebes, ruddy ducks, goldeneye and all the other usual suspects.

To access the property requires some careful wiggling under barbed wire unless you can locate a gate. It appears that nobody minds walkers so long as they are respectful of the place. I have trekked to the end of the lake without encountering a No Trespassing notice. Beyond this point would seem to be intruding on the ranch and possibly a First Nations Reserve.

The "mission" in Mission Ponds is a reference to the Saint Joseph's Mission, established by the Oblate Fathers in the San Jose Valley south of the city in 1866.

Mission Ponds wetlands.

45. *FOX MOUNTAIN TRAIL*

Easy hike, moderate/advanced bike
Distance 6.5-km hike to Signal Point;
13-km bike circle route
Duration 1.5-hour hike Signal Point
1.5-hour bike circle route;
Maximum elevation **880 m**
Elevation loss 180 m
Map **93 B/1** Williams Lake

Access: Take Highway 97 north 2.5 km and turn right onto Fox Mountain Road. Watch for the gas pipeline 2.5 km along on the left. Across from this is an unnamed gravel road. Park here. The trailhead is a few metres in on the south side of the road.

Fox Mountain offers pleasant woodland walking interspersed with great viewpoints of the lake, Scout Island and the Sugar Cane Reserve to the south.

The powerline section, about one third of the trail, is unatractive for walkers. I would recommend one of three options for walkers. Option one is to walk in 3 km, take in the various viewpoints and return the same way. Option two is to walk as far as Signal Point and return the same way, a 13-km round trip. Finally, you can park one vehicle at Signal Point and another at the trailhead. Signal Point is the rocky bluff just above the highway on the way south. It is reached via the trailer court on Coleman Road, a block or two south of McDonalds. Park at the top of the road. Walk to the point for the view then return to the power line and take the narrow right-hand trail from there heading south down the lake. Follow this to the Fox Mountain trailhead.

46. SCOUT ISLAND NATURE CENTRE

Short, easy walks
Map 93 B/1 Williams Lake

Access: South on Highway 20 to Mackenzie Avenue and left to Borland Drive, Scout Island is on the right off Borland.

Scout Island is a pleasant oasis located on two islands at the west end of the lake, close to the industrial area. It is an interesting spot to while away a few hours and is especially suited to families. In addition to the conservation and educational aspects, there is a sandy beach and a play area.

Interpretive walking trails lead the visitor to various observation locations and the Nature Centre, where you can learn about the flora and fauna of the marshes and islands and admire the view down the lake. For a longer hike, Scout Island is the start of the 14-km-long Williams Lake River Valley trail.

47. WILLIAMS LAKE RIVER VALLEY TRAIL

Easy hike, bike
Distance 14 km total; 4 km from trailhead
Duration 2.75 hours
Map 93 B/1 Williams Lake & River Valley trail map

Access: South on Highway 20, there are a number of access points off Mackenzie Avenue. One option, suitable for mountain biking is to park at the Turbo station on the left just north of the BC Rail station. A road to the left crosses the railway tracks and leads down to the valley. From here it is 11.5 km to the trail end. The most popular access for walkers is 4 km north on Mackenzie Avenue, left onto Soda Creek Road and an immediate left onto Frizzi Road, crossing the railway tracks. Turn right and proceed along this road, past the

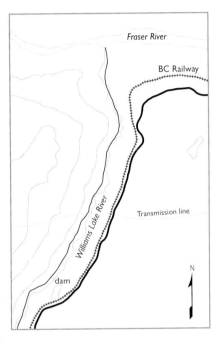

landfill and through the industrial area. The pavement narrows to gravel and switchbacks down to the valley bottom. Once there, continue along for 1 km, and head to the right at the fork to access the trailhead.

Following decades of abuse during which industrial and domestic garbage was dumped – legally and illegally – above and into the valley, a few determined individuals began the long process of restoration. They convinced clubs, politicians and governments to get involved in creating a beautiful recreation corridor extending from Scout Island 14 km to the Fraser River.

It has to be admitted that some parts of the completed trail are not that attractive. The south end is visually unappealing, passing as it does by an industrial section and a sewage plant. Vehicles are permitted up to a point 5 km from the end; after that, only hikers and cyclists have access. From there on, the scenery is outstanding.

With its amazing diversity of plant and bird life, the valley is a naturalist's paradise. Black cottonwoods, Douglas fir and white birch are found along the way, and the numerous habitats ranging from stream, marsh, forest, grasslands and spectacular sandy cliffs attract a great many species of birds. Pygmy owls and goshawks make the valley their year-round home. Great blue herons inhabit the marshy areas. The more remote western end of the valley is visited by black bear, bobcat, moose and mule deer. Muskrat and mink live along the riverbank and beaver are very active: chewed birch stumps and lodges, both active and abandoned, abound along the riverbank. To really appreciate the varied wildlife calls for an unhurried approach with frequent side trips to view activity on the river.

The first-time visitor is never prepared for the dramatic end to the trail: one minute in forest and the next on the shores of the rushing Fraser River, into which the Williams Lake River empties. It is an appropriate and awe-inspiring conclusion.

Trail Trivia

Number of bridges installed along the Williams Lake River Valley trail: 20. They are actually recycled BC Rail boxcar decks.

Numbers of truckloads of garbage removed from the valley by the 2nd Williams Lake Brownie Pack and other youth groups on May 15, 1993: two.

Number of discarded tires removed from the creek and valley: an estimated 1,500.

Other species of debris removed include industrial concrete, railway ties, truck and auto bodies and tonnes of glass, cans and plastic.

Prior to the cleanup, a storm sewer emptied into the creek.

Fish now spawning in the cleaned-up river include rainbow trout and an annual run of pink salmon from the Fraser.

Number of bird species seen in the valley at various times: more than two hundred.

Project cost: close to $500,000.

Bull Mountain Trails

48. *CARIBOO WOODLOT EDUCATION SOCIETY TRAILS*

Easy walks
Distances 2 and 3 km
Durations 0.5 and 0.75 hour
Map 93 B/1 Williams Lake

Access: Turn left onto Bull Mountain Road 18 km north of Williams Lake on Highway 97. The woodlot sign is on the right a short way up. The trails start from there.

Two walks comprise the society's trails: the 3-km Silviculture Trail and the shorter Minton Creek walk. Both are attractive woodland walks. The emphasis is on flora and fauna identification and forest appreciation.

Minton Creek woodland walk.

101

49. BULL MOUNTAIN SKI TRAILS (SUMMER ACCESS)

Easy/moderate hikes
Distance 2.5-, 5-, 8- and 12-km loops
Duration 0.5 to 3 hours
Maximum elevation 1050 m
Map 93 B/1 Williams Lake & Bull Mountain ski trails map

Access: See previous hike, #48. The summer access is across the road from the woodlot trail and just a few metres to the left of the barrier to the ski trails parking lot

The Bull Mountain trails offer variety in distance and terrain, from a short meadow and pond loop to longer forest hikes. The trails are well-signed and maps are available online or from the Williams Lake Visitor Centre.

Meadow trail, Bull Mountain.

Horsefly and Likely Area

When the Cariboo Wagon Road skirted Williams Lake, 150 Mile House became an important junction. Here freight and passengers transferred to stagecoaches heading to the Chilcotin or to the goldfields at Horsefly and Likely. Today there is very little sign of that former prominence, except that it is from here that the road runs east to where the first Cariboo gold was discovered, on the Horsefly River. Recognizable hiking trails are few in the flat to rolling ranch country between Williams Lake and Horsefly, but the more rugged terrain east of Likely offers some fine mountain hiking.

Horsefly

The intriguing name supposedly stems from the biting reception the gold seekers received from the local insect population. The strike thought to have propelled the Cariboo gold rush was made here by Peter Dunlevy and four friends, led by Long Baptiste, their Shuswap guide. The group panned their first pay dirt on the banks of the Horsefly River in June 1859. Although the miners subsequently moved to richer creeks farther north, Horsefly remained an important ranching and supply centre. Today, this tiny community is associated with the second-largest sockeye salmon run in the province, one that has seen as many as a million fish. The sockeye run starts toward the end of August. Mid-September is the best time to view these brilliant red-and-green spawners in the channels. A trail on the east side of the river by the bridge goes a little way upstream to enable visitors and locals alike to see the fish.

Overlooking Horsefly Lake, Horsefly Provincial Park.

Horsefly River.

50. *HORSEFLY LAKE PROVINCIAL PARK LOOKOUT*

Easy hike

Distance 500 m

Maximum elevation 835 m

Elevation gain 40 m

Map 93A Quesnel Lake

Access: From 150 Mile House, 10 km south of Williams Lake, take the Horsefly–Likely road 60 km west to Horsefly. Across the bridge, turn right 13 km along a good gravel road to the park.

As it doesn't provide much of a hike in terms of distance, this walk is best combined with hike #51, Viewland Mountain. The two can easily be completed in the same day. To miss the lookout is to miss one of the prettiest little walks in the area.

The trail is not immediately apparent from the parking lot. You need to walk toward the biffies to locate the trail on the left, identified by a sign explaining that a fire in 1936 destroyed all but two of the original great Douglas firs and that all the firs located in the park today are offspring of those two giants. Trembling aspen have sprung up in place of the burned fir. Their slimness and spacing allows considerable light penetration, and this coupled with the leafy green carpeting of low salmonberry makes for a delightful woodland walk.

The summit offers superb views of Horsefly Lake, one of the most beautiful in the Cariboo. In addition, a number of short "unofficial" paths lead down and along the ridge to additional fine viewpoints. These fairly steep trails require caution and good footwear.

51. *VIEWLAND MOUNTAIN*

Easy hike
Distance 4 km
Duration 1 hour
Maximum elevation 1325 m
Elevation gain 365 m
Map 93A Quesnel Lake

Access: From Horsefly, drive 22 km on Horsefly Lake Road to Viewland Creek Forest Road on the right. The trailhead is 1.3 km along this road on the right. Should you come to a logged area, you have gone too far. Retrace about 20 m. When last visited, the sign identifying the trail was facing away, so you may have to walk the road a bit to locate the access.

The trail to Viewland Mountain is a well-maintained, fairly easy walk through a forest of Douglas fir, some cedar and, in the lower reaches, towering cottonwood. False Solomon's seal and false box provide much of the thick groundcover. On top, the mountain lives up to its name, providing an excellent panorama despite the clear-cut blocks visible on all sides. To the northeast you can see all the way down the north arm of Quesnel Lake – largest in the Cariboo at 100 km in length and as deep as 610 m – to the snow-covered peaks of the Cariboo Mountains, Mitchell/Niagara Provincial Park and, directly east, to Wells Gray Provincial Park. Horsefly Lake is the large body of water to the south.

Likely

The settlement of Likely is situated north of Horsefly at the west end of Quesnel Lake on the mouth of the Quesnel River. Originally known as "Quesnel Dam," the name was changed in 1923 in honour of "Plato John" Likely, one of the first prospectors in the area and considered something of a philosopher. The area retains a strong sense of the gold rush. The ghost town of Quesnel Forks, once a lively town of 5,000, with the largest Chinese community in North America, is located 8 km past Likely. The Bullion Pit Mine on Sharpe Road, 4 km west of Likely, is one of the world's largest man-made canyons – more than 3 km long and 92 m wide. In its first six years of operation the mine yielded $1.25-million worth of gold, and in 1938 it was using more water per day than the entire city of Vancouver. Mining, which began in 1892, continued until 1942, with some renewed activity in 1984. Although cattle ranching and tourism have replaced mining as the principal economic activities today, high metals prices have sparked active exploratory work in the area recently, and some individual placer holdings are still being worked.

Fisheries inspection vessel, Quesnel River, Likely.

52. *CAMERON RIDGE TRAIL*

Easy hike
Distance 7 km from road
Duration 2 hours
Maximum elevation 1150 m
Elevation gain 330 m
Map 93 A/15 Mitchell Lake

Access: From 150 Mile east to Likely. Follow Keithly Creek Road from Likely (all but 5 km is gravel) for 20 km to the Barkerville turnoff. Turn right across the bridge and left onto the 8400 logging road for 50 km to the Little River mining road on the right. Park on the

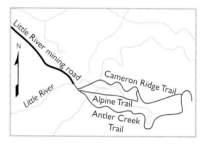

shoulder. There is some washboard along 8400 Road, but it is perfectly driveable and does not require four-wheel drive.

There is a considerable amount of driving involved to reach this location, but it is worth it. From mid-July to the end of August the wildflowers are a treat: Indian paintbrush in that rich red shade found at higher elevations, purple aster, heliotrope, fireweed and sunny arnica line the trail and colour the meadows. Heather grows higher up. The view from the ridge of the oxbows of the Mitchell River Wetlands 300 m below is unequalled. The trail was first created in 1963 by members of the Cariboo Wilderness Coalition to draw attention to the spectacular, wildlife-rich watershed of the Penfold Valley, whose ancient cedar and spruce forests were threatened by logging road construction. The area has since been incorporated into Cariboo Mountains Park.

The first 4 km of the hike utilizes the Little River mining road. There are signs of former mining exploration at various locations along the way: mounds of quartz, some rusting machinery, small quarries. The ridge trail materializes on the left where a little stream cuts across the road.

From here it's a winding hike to the ridge, mainly through Engelmann spruce, interspersed with lovely subalpine flower meadows. On last hiking it, I found a downhill stretch of the trail blocked by blowdowns necessitating some bushwhacking and detouring around. Just before the ridge lookout, a sign indicates a path to a viewpoint above Mitchell Lake. It is worth the short diversion to take in the view.

Instead of descending by the same route, there is an even lovelier way the Antler Spring Trail, which loops back to the Little River mining road. What makes this Antler trail so attractive are the many small and larger outcroppings and ponds of various sizes. Purple and white heather grow here, together with columbine and wild rhododendron.

As you leave the ridge, about 500 m along, a sign indicates Antler Spring Trail to the left. The signs are becoming harder to locate, however, as the trees they originally were tacked onto have grown much taller and carried the signs upward with them. The Antler trail meets up with the mining road after 2 km. From here it is 6 km back to 8400 Road for a round trip of 15 km via Antler Spring.

A note: This area is frequented by both black and grizzly bears. We saw evidence of the former but didn't see any bears. It is probably advisable to keep your presence well announced.

Flower meadows, Cameron Ridge Trail.

53. *CAMERON RIDGE ALPINE MEADOWS*

Easy/moderate hike
Distance 8.5 km from 8400 Road
Duration 2+ hours
Max elevation 1825 m
Elevation gain 550 m
Map 93 A/15 Mitchell Lake

Access: See Cameron Ridge Trail.

This trail leads to the right of and higher than the Cameron Ridge viewpoint, to an alpine meadow offering the same dramatic views as the other but in a more open area without Cameron's sheer drop-off.

Instead of turning left at the stream to the Cameron Ridge lookout, continue uphill on the quad track through the stream gully and through the meadow above it. From here the track winds left for a stretch then veers right to the alpine. It is a relatively easy hike with steep sections at the start and finish. This less-forested route allows more unobscured views of Mount Matthew and other spectacular Cariboo mountain peaks.

Cameron Ridge viewpoint.

54. EUREKA MEADOWS

Easy/moderate hike
Distance 5 km
Duration 1.5 hours
Maximum elevation 2100 m (Repeater)
Elevation gain 600 m
Map 93 A/2 McKinley Creek

Access: From Williams Lake, go 15 km south and 60 km east to Horsefly. From Horsefly, go right (east) for 45 km on Black Creek Road. At Crooked Lake fork keep left on 100 Road (Black Creek Road) and continue just over 5 km to Whiskey Bridges. The road and bridge are on the right. At 5.2 km from the bridge go left, and 0.5 km after this go left again. Another 0.5 km along keep right. Look for a large steel tripod on a tree on your right. This is the end of the driven part.

A long drive along hot dusty roads doesn't sound like fun, but all the effort is worth it for the gorgeous displays of wildflowers, matching that of the Trophy Mountains in Wells Gray Park. If that isn't enough, the views from the ridge up to and beyond the repeater station are magnificent.

This is a hike best done in a group. Getting to the meadows can be a little tricky. The paths have become quite overgrown, so it helps to go with someone who is familiar with the area. Thankfully, I had members of the Williams Lake Field Naturalists to show me the way. The trailhead for the route they chose is directly across the road from the triangle marker and is barely distinguishable due to vegetation encroachment. It obviously doesn't see much use. If you can locate this, however, it eventually opens up and becomes a decent trail switchbacking up through the forest before breaking out into a series of meadows and finally open alpine meadow. From here, watch for ribbon markers on trees marking the route through the meadow in the direction of the ridge. The repeater tower will now be obvious on your right.

Should you be unable to locate the access trail as described, perhaps continuing ahead beyond the marker will offer another route up.

Above Eureka Meadows.

Looking down on Farwell Canyon and the Chilcotin River.

The descent to Dante's Inferno (hike #58)

Merging of the Fraser and Chilcotin Rivers from the Junction Sheep Range.

Eastern Chilcotin

Highway 20, The "Freedom Highway," which cuts across the Chilcotin Plateau west of Williams Lake, is the ribbon of access to thousands of square kilometres of potentially great hiking country, as well as to established trail networks such as those existing in Tweedsmuir Park and Ts'il?os Provincial Park. These parks, however, are located at the coastal end of the Chilcotin, nearly 400 km from Williams Lake and well beyond the scope of this guide. The eastern part of the Chilcotin remains largely untapped and unmapped as far as trails are concerned. Still, there are a few locations within reasonable driving distance of the city and endless room to roam and discover others.

Fraser River benchland, Old Meldrum Creek Road Trail.

114

55. OLD MELDRUM CREEK ROAD TRAIL

Easy hike, bike

Distances 4 to 25 km

Durations 1- to 6-hour hike; 0.25- to 2.5-hour bike

Map 92 O/16 Alkali Lake

Access: Take Highway 20 from Williams Lake for 26 km, crossing the Fraser on Sheep Creek Bridge and continuing 1.2 km uphill. Look for an access on the right and a gated road with Private No Trespassing signs. This is a public road; the signs refer to private ranch property on either side of the road for the first two kilometres. You can park and hike from the gate, or, with a high-centred vehicle, drive another 2 km to a parking spot off trail left.

The Old Meldrum Creek Road is named for Thomas Meldrum, the first white man to permanently settle in the Chilcotin. The road is 25 km long and heads north through forest for the most part, along the Fraser River benches to Rudy Johnson Bridge on Old Soda Creek Road north of Williams Lake. Its length renders it suited to mountain biking, but walkers can bite off a section of any length and take in the superb views of the Fraser River offered by occasionally veering off the trail at open patches on the right. At about the 7 km mark from the gate, there is evidence of Chinese prospecting activity in the years following the gold rushes. A sign indicates a ditch running from the bluffs on the left and across the road into the trees right. The ditch was likely used to bring water down to the prospectors' claim sites, where they washed the gravel to extract any gold

56. *DOC ENGLISH BLUFF*

Easy, short but steep hike
Distance 1 km
Duration 0.25 hour
Maximum elevation 690 m
Elevation gain 50 m
Map 92 0/16 Alkali Lake

Access: Via Highway 20 from Williams Lake. At about 30 km watch for Moon Road on the left just before a steep winding climb below the lookout point. The bluff is located about 3 km along Moon Road on the left. Park at what looks like a gravel pit under the bluff.

Named after one Benjamin Franklin "Doc" English, a pioneer prospector/trader who settled in the area, the bluff is located on the Deer Ranch Wildlife Reserve. The reserve is linked to the junction Sheep Range Wildlife Reserve to the southwest. As a

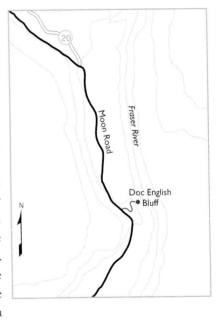

sign at the entrance to Moon Road indicates, the bluff itself is an ecological reserve protecting unique flora and also white-throated swifts and golden eagles, rarely seen in the Cariboo–Chilcotin. The hike to the top takes less than 15 minutes, but the trail is steep and requires caution. From the top of the bluff there are magnificent views of the Fraser River 330 m below and the ranchlands on the benches opposite. As an added bonus there are caves. Like the climb up, these are short and almost vertical. In his journey of 1808 down the river that bears his name, Simon Fraser appears to have recorded these same caves in his journal when he refers to "a hill of shape like an old castle" and to a "long and dangerous rapid which is called Rapid du Trou from a hole that appears in the perpendicular rock on the right side."

Farther along Deer Ranch Road, just before the ranch itself, you may be lucky enough to spot long-billed curlews in the fields on either side.

The Fraser River, looking north from Doc English Bluff.

57. THE DOME

Easy hike

Distance 5 km

Duration 1.5 hour

Maximum elevation 1378 m

Elevation gain 325 m

Maps 92 O/15 Riske Creek and 93 B/2 Drummond Lake

Access: Take Highway 20 to Riske Creek. Turn right onto Stack Road just after Chilcotin Lodge. Fourteen km along Stack Road there is a road on the left, apparently Badger Road but without a sign identifying it as such. It is better to note the forestry numbers on poles. The trailhead is at #134.

The Dome, which is clearly of volcanic origin, is the highest point on the landscape and presents outstanding views of Becher's Prairie and the Coast

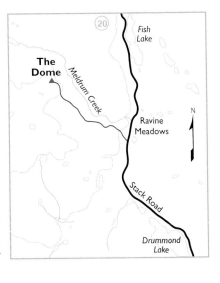

Mountains. The length of the hike depends on where you start walking from. It is possible to drive a considerable length of the road with a high-centred vehicle. The route is straightforward for the most part. Keep to the right wherever the road forks.

58. DANTE'S INFERNO (CRATER LAKE)

Easy hike

Distance 4 km

Duration: I hour

Map 92 0/15 Riske Creek

Access: On Highway 20 from Williams Lake, go 68.5 km to Beaumont Road on the left. Drive 1.4 km on Beaumont to where a dirt road intersects on the right. Continue right another 3.5 km and park where the stream cuts through the meadow. Cross the stream and follow the trail alongside the fence

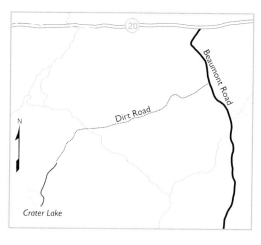

to the corrals. Continue left and down through the forest to lake.

Dante's Inferno, aka Crater Lake, is one of a series of small parks and protected areas in the Cariboo–Chilcotin. An eroded canyon with basaltic formation, it is a smaller version of another Crater Lake east of 70 Mile House in the Cariboo. To see more of the lake and the grasslands above the Chilcotin River beyond the park boundary, return uphill from the lake a short way and take the path heading right and down to the eastern shore of the lake. If you climb back up from the lake here and look southwest, you will be looking down on the grassy benchlands above the Chilcotin River. Simply pick the line of least resistance downhill, which will involve some bushwhacking, until you reach the ranch road running east to west. If you head right (west) toward the riparian zone, you will discover a prominent group of kekulis (Native pit houses) located on the left just above the stream. The dwellings are estimated to be around two hundred years old.

59. THE JUNCTION SHEEP RANGE

Easy hiking, biking
Distances up to 15 km
Durations up to 4 hours
Maximum elevation 960 m
Elevation gain 75 m
Maps 92 0/15 Riske Creek and 92 0/16 Alkali Lake

Access: Take Highway 20 to Riske Creek. Go south 15 km on Farwell Canyon Road. The range is signed on the left. There is a parking area just off the road.

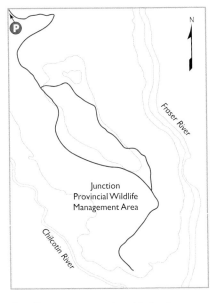

The Junction Sheep Range is home to the largest herd of California bighorn sheep on the continent and is an area of dramatic beauty. It is possible to drive all the way through to a point overlooking where the Fraser River and the Chilcotin River merge to the Gang Ranch, and hike or bike the trails from there. The road, however, is a real roller coaster and a high-clearance vehicle is essential. Starting from the parking lot, hikers and mountain bikers have many options to explore branch trails off the road or walk to the benchlands on the right above the Chilcotin River.

Depending on the time of year, bighorn sheep can be seen in the canyons and on the benchlands on the west side of the range. BC Parks visitor information signs at points along the road provide detailed information on the flora and fauna of the area.

Farwell Canyon

Centuries before the first white settlers began to drift into the Chilcotin, this site on the banks of the rushing Chilcotin River was a seasonal Native village. Here the Chilcotin people constructed their kekuli, or keekwillies: underground winter dwellings made of logs insulated with sod, pine needles and branches. Evidence of the pithouses can still be detected in a series of circular depressions that are becoming increasingly overgrown with shrubs and grasses.

In the summer months, the descendants of the kekuli-dwellers carry on the tradition of netting salmon and drying them in the traditional way on racks at their campsites.

As a scenic attraction, Farwell is a remarkable place. The glacial-blue river cuts through the canyon in a series of oxbows. Above, erosion has left hoodoos, or free-standing sandstone formations, on the steep slopes and created a remarkable 300-m sand dune high above the river.

To the left of the abandoned Canyon Ranch buildings, a road leads down to the bridge, to the right of which a path leads to some pictographs.

Farwell Canyon hoodoos.

Farwell Canyon. The sand dune is on the right.

60. FARWELL CANYON SAND DUNE

Easy/moderate hike
Distance 1–2 km
Elevation gain 50 m
Map 92 0/15 Riske Creek

Access: See the Junction Sheep Range hike, #59. Continue downhill past Sheep Junction to the km 19 marker on the right. Drive in and park. The trail is on the right, downhill to start. The dune can also be accessed farther downhill just before the bridge. Using the latter route, park on the left, walk across the road and uphill about 60 m. The path is on the left. Look for it

in the scrub. It is a steep downhill and uphill to the dune.

The Farwell Canyon sand dune has been featured in *Beautiful British Columbia* magazine as "one of the seven wonders of the West." Since then, BC photographer/publisher Chris Harris has added to its fame by featuring it in his book on the Cariboo–Chilcotin called *Spirit in the Grass*.

The route from the parking lot at km 19 begins with a descent into an arroyo, followed by another, before climbing around and up to the grasslands. From there it is an easy walk left to the dune.

61. *FARWELL CANYON RIDGE*

Easy/moderate hike
Distance 5 km
Duration 1.25 hour
Elevation 800 m
Elevation gain 180 m
Map 92 0/15 Riske Creek
GPS 51.50N, 122.33 W

Access: See the previous hike and Junction Sheep Range, #59. Start at km 19 marker.

From this higher elevation there are spectacular views of the canyon over 1,000 feet (305 m) below and to the Junction Sheep Range and beyond to the east.

After the trail climbs out of the arroyos and onto the flat,

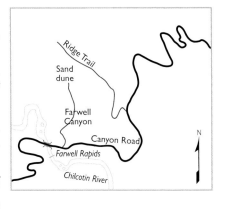

rather than heading left toward the dune, continue through the grassland toward the hoodoos. Then look for the trail veering right to the ridge. Nearer the top there is a choice of tracks; take any that head uphill. Once on the ridge there is no end of possibilities for extending the hike. Proceeding left to the end of the ridge looking in the direction of the parking area, drop down into the gully and then head left. A short walk through this wooded gully leads to a meadow in which is situated a large weathered balancing rock. From the ridge, heading right, there are hikes to be explored: a climb to the next ridge or a walk westward to see more of the river canyon, with the possibility of spotting bighorn sheep on the canyon trails and benchlands.

Cross-country Ski Trails

The Cariboo offers a number of cross-country ski trail networks between Clinton and Williams Lake. The 99 Mile and 108 community trail networks are the most extensive and longest-established in the region.

Scenic Sucker Lake trail #14, 108 ski trails.

Snow Conditions

Snow conditions can be as varied as winter itself in the Cariboo, with more snow some years than others. Severe cold is rare and tends to last only a few days. A temperature range of −15 to 10°C is fairly typical. Perfect conditions occur when there is lots of snow, the mercury is in the −5 to −10° range, the trails have just been set, the sky is blue and your long underwear doesn't droop.

Clothing

The experienced Nordic skier knows how to dress for the conditions and can usually spot a beginner a kilometre away by his silhouette: somewhere between a pack mule and a polar explorer. Beginners tend to overdress. Cross-country skiing provides a great workout, and the best approach is to dress in layers that can be peeled off if necessary as you warm up. Hooded parkas, baggy pants and a rucksack may be fine for backcountry shuffling, but on groomed trails they amount to a portable sauna. If you want to do it right, shun cotton and invest in quality polypropylene, which wicks away the moisture. Cotton has the opposite effect: it soaks up moisture and may cause the wearer to become quite chilled.

Food and Drink

You should carry liquid as a matter of course. A waist-fitting water bottle holder or the increasingly popular camelpack that permits sipping without stopping are the most convenient containers. For nourishment, energy bars that can be easily slipped into a pocket are handy items. If you are planning to make a morning or afternoon of it and just amble around taking in the scenery, you probably will want to stuff more than this into a light day pack.

Sucker Lake trail.

BIG BAR SKI TRAILS, CLINTON

Access: Ten km north of Clinton, turn left onto Big Bar Road. The trails are located 6 km along on the left.

When the Big Bar trails were first developed, they were well-used and well-maintained, and there was an active club membership. In recent years, interest and maintenance appear to have declined. At the time of writing, trails were still being set by snowmobile although not packed. A particularly attractive section of the Big Bar trails is on the southwest side, with wonderful outlooks to the snow-capped Marble Mountains.

To check on conditions at the Big Bar trails, contact the Clinton Snow Jockey Club, 250-459-7751, or Parkie's Store, 250-459-2335.

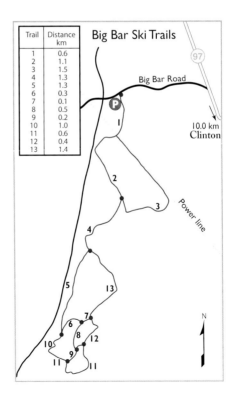

Trail	Distance km
1	0.6
2	1.1
3	1.5
4	1.3
5	1.3
6	0.3
7	0.1
8	0.5
9	0.2
10	1.0
11	0.6
12	0.4
13	1.4

Big Bar Ski Trails

THE 99 MILE SKI TRAILS

This perfectly groomed network of trails south of 100 Mile House was constructed to international racing standards to enable the community to host major events, such as the Canadian Junior Championships and Masters competitions. Overall, the system is technically challenging, although touring bypasses have been constructed around some of the steeper sections, and the 10-km touring route accommodates the intermediate and less-experienced skier. Beginner Jackrabbits learn their technique on the flat 1-km oval and on the children's adventure trail. The 99 Mile trails are also home to the annual 50-km Cariboo Marathon Cross-country Ski Race.

There are two lighted circuits of 2.5 and 3.5 km. The lights remain on between 4:30 and 9:00 pm. A fine log day lodge is located in the stadium.

Ski passes, either for the season or for day use, are required at all area trails and can be purchased at the 108 Hills resort and the Red Coach Inn. An honour box is also provided for day-use donations.

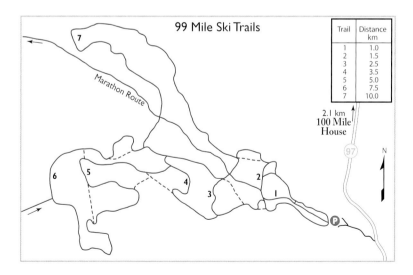

99 Mile Ski Trails

Trail	Distance km
1	1.0
2	1.5
3	2.5
4	3.5
5	5.0
6	7.5
7	10.0

Marathon Route

2.1 km
100 Mile House

THE 108 COMMUNITY SKI TRAIL NETWORK

The most scenic and varied ski trails in the region and some of the best in the province are located in the area encompassing the 108 Hills Health Ranch and various rights-of-way east of the 108 Mile Ranch subdivision. It all adds up to around 100 km of superb Nordic skiing on expertly groomed trails tracked for both classic and skating styles.

The 108 ski trails can be accessed from a number of locations: from The 108 Hills Health Ranch, The 108 Resort, the tunnel under Highway 97 behind the Turbo gas station, and the tunnel under the highway opposite the 108 Heritage Site. Parking is available at all four locations.

Trail Lengths and Classification

A map of the 108 network is included in this section and can be obtained from either of the resorts. It is not a bad idea to carry one if you haven't skied the area before. The same maps enlarged and with "you are here" symbols are posted at key trail intersections. The maps are colour-coded to identify each trail's level of difficulty. Distances on the map represent one-way only, as opposed to the combination loops described here, which give the total round-trip distances. While the maps posted on the trails provide a pretty good sense of where you are in the system, they are in need of updating and may not always correspond with what you see. Some trails have been rerouted; others no longer groomed.

Trail Facilities

At three different locations on the 108 network there are day cabins where tired or hungry skiers can stop to rest or snack. At last count, two were equipped with wood-burning stoves. These are not meant for overnight use. There are no outhouses along the system. Something has to be left to individual creativity!

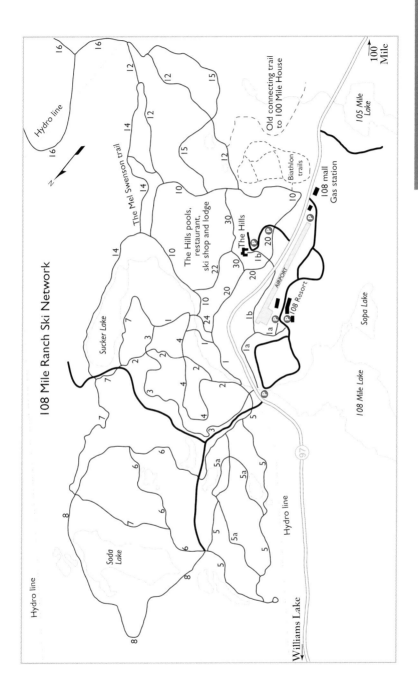

108 Mile Ranch Ski Network

131

Trail Fees

Day passes can be purchased at The 108 Hills Health Ranch and The 108 Resort. Season passes are available from the 108 Hills or the 100 Mile Nordics.

The 108 Hills Network

A number of short trails winding through the forest at The 108 Hills Health Ranch provide the beginner cross-country skier an opportunity to become comfortable on skinny skis before tackling some of the lengthier trails beyond. Trails #20–28, 30, 31 and 61–67 are easy trails ranging from 0.3 to 3.4 km. Connector trails from the Hills meet up with perimeter trails and others of the community trails system. The pages following illustrate just some of the many possible combinations utilizing the two networks. They are selected to provide a sampling of shorter and longer routes. Durations are on the generous side to allow for a range of abilities.

Great skiing at the 108!

62. *COMBINATION TRAILS 1, 24, 1*

Easy
Distance 5 km
Duration 1 hour

Access: The underpass opposite the 108 Heritage Site.

There are two possibilities with this route, depending on how experienced a skier you are. Novices may feel more comfortable undertaking it in reverse and opt for a climb at the beginning rather than a downhill stretch at the end. Beyond this it is an easy route.

From the tunnel, turn right and follow trail #1, ignoring any branches on the right until the trail swings right across a dike to the intersection of trails #10 and 24. Turn right on #24, and proceed uphill to another intersection, at which point head right and onto trail #1 heading left. This will bring you back to the underpass.

63. *COMBINATION TRAILS 10 AND 20*

Easy
Distance 7.5 km
Duration 1.3 hours

Access: From the Hills Resort or via the underpass at the Turbo station.

This combination sees a lot of use by all classes of skier. It is usually the first of the season to be groomed. It has a nice variety of terrain: ups, downs and fast flat stretches. Mostly in the trees, it is not quite as scenic as some of the outlying routes, perhaps, but given a fresh mantle of snow, this can be a lovely ski. There is only one hill, more of a bump, that requires herringboning.

64. COMBINATION TRAILS 10, 11, 14, 7, 1 AND 20

Easy/intermediate
Distance 15 km
Duration 2 hours

Access: See previous combination.

Other than its length, and some climbing and winding downhill on the trail #1 sector, this combination presents few challenges to the average skier. It is an attractive route with a variety of terrain and a cabin on trail #1 for a chow break.

65. PERIMETER TRAIL COMBO

Intermediate
Distance 25 km
Duration 3 hours

Access: Via the underpass opposite 108 Heritage Site. Head uphill on trail #5.

This route includes "outside" trails #5, 6, 9, 7, 14 and 12, the most scenic trails in the network, incorporating forest, lakeshore and meadow. Trails #10 and 24 complete the circle on the homeward stretch. Classified overall as intermediate because of its length, this is not a particularly technical route and can be undertaken by most fit and experienced skiers. There is a bit of climbing at the start, and some downhill on trails #5 and #6. There is a nice wilderness feel to the route, as you encounter few other skiers for long stretches on the back sections.

66. *BULL MOUNTAIN SKI TRAILS (WILLIAMS LAKE)*

Rating easy, intermediate, difficult.

Access: Drive 18 km north of Williams Lake and turn left on Bull Mountain Road. Drive 1 km.

The Bull Mountain site, managed by the Williams Lake Cross-country Ski Club, comprises 28 km of trails of 3, 5, 8 and 12 km varying from beginner to advanced, with 3.5 km of lighted trails and a warming hut. The trails are nicely groomed, well-signed and colour-coded. The club has an active Jackrabbit program. Day-use fees are $10.

Skiers, Bull Mountain trails.

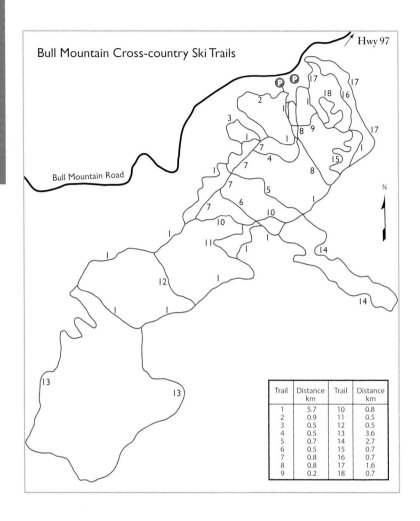

Bull Mountain Cross-country Ski Trails

Hwy 97

Bull Mountain Road

N

Trail	Distance km	Trail	Distance km
1	5.7	10	0.8
2	0.9	11	0.5
3	0.5	12	0.5
4	0.5	13	3.6
5	0.7	14	2.7
6	0.5	15	0.7
7	0.8	16	0.7
8	0.8	17	1.6
9	0.2	18	0.7

References

The following publications were invaluable in providing historical, geological, natural history and other background information about the region.

Books

Bryan, Liz & Jack Bryan. *Backroads of British Columbia*. Vancouver: Sunflower Books, 1975.

Downs, Art. *Wagon Road North: Saga of the Cariboo Gold Rush*. Surrey, BC: Heritage House, 1987.

Downs, Art, ed. *Cariboo Gold Rush*. Surrey, BC: Heritage House Publishing, 1994.

Harris, Chris. *Spirit in the Grass: The Cariboo–Chilcotin's Forgotten Landscape*. 108 Mile Ranch, BC: Country Light Publishing, 2007.

Neave, Roland. *Exploring Wells Gray Park*, 4th ed. Kamloops, BC: The Friends of Wells Gray Park, 1995.

Patenaude, Branwen. *Trails to Gold*, vol. 2. Surrey, BC: Heritage House, 1996.

Roberts, J.A. *Cariboo. A Brief History*. Williams Lake, BC: Williams Lake Public Library, 1986.

Stangoe, Irene. *Cariboo–Chilcotin Pioneer People & Places*. Surrey, BC: Heritage House, 1994.

Unpublished pamphlets, booklets

Hornby, Chris. Ten Walks in Williams Lake.

Neilans et al. A Brief History of Williams Lake.

Other Published

Excerpted material, Marble Range. Vancouver: Geoscience Research Library.

In addition to the above, the "morgue" at the 100 Mile House Free Press includes a collection of back issues of *Cariboo Calling*, an annual magazine about Cariboo pioneers and the history of Cariboo communities. These proved a most valuable resource to me while writing, as did various BC Parks, South Cariboo Tourism and Cariboo–Chilcotin Tourism publications.

Index

Mountain Footsteps
Hikes in the East Kootenay of Southeastern British Columbia
Third Edition

Janice Strong

Mountain Footsteps is one of Rocky Mountain Books' bestselling hiking guides. Covering routes around Cranbrook, Kimberley, Creston, Invermere, Radium and Fernie, located between the Rocky Mountains in the east and the Purcell Mountains in the west – including the Akamina Kishinena, Top of the World, Elk Lakes, St. Mary's Alpine and Bugaboo Glacier Provincial parks – this volume will entice hikers of all abilities.

ISBN 978-1-897522-43-1
Colour Photos, Maps
$26.95, Softcover

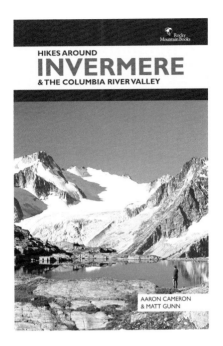

HIKES AROUND INVERMERE
& the Columbia River Valley

Aaron Cameron and Matt Gunn

From short strolls to dayhikes to overnighters to major, committing moun-
taineering routes, *Hikes Around Invermere* has all the information you
need to get out there and enjoy the most beautiful spots at Spillimacheen
River, Horsethief, Toby and Frances creeks, Mount Assiniboine, the
Stanford Range, the Bugaboos, Kootenay National Park and Height of
the Rockies.

ISBN 978-1-897522-51-6
B/W Photos, Maps
$19.95, Softcover

About the Author

Colin Campbell is a retired teacher/librarian. He lived at the historic 108 Mile Ranch, in the heart of the Southern Cariboo region of British Columbia, surrounded by rolling hills, thousands of lakes and a wide range of recreational activities. He regularly explores, hikes, skis and bikes the routes featured in this book.